The New Keynesian Macroeconomics

To SBTDB

The New Keynesian Macroeconomics

Time, Belief and Social Interdependence

Shaun P. Hargreaves Heap
School of Economic and Social Studies
University of East Anglia

Edward Elgar

Published by
Edward Elgar Publishing Limited
Gower House
Croft Road
Aldershot
Hants GU11 3HR
England

Edward Elgar Publishing Limited
Distributed in the United States by
Ashgate Publishing Company
Old Post Road
Brookfield
Vermont 05036
USA

A CIP catalogue record for this book
is available from the British Library

Library of Congress Cataloging-in-Publication Data
Heap, Shaun Hargreaves, 1951–
    The new Keynesian macroeconomics: time, belief, and social
interdependence/by Shaun P. Hargreaves Heap.
        p. cm.
    Includes index.
    1. Keynesian economics. 2. Macroeconomics. I. Title.
HB99.7.H43 1992
330.15′6–dc20   91–28758
                                                                                    CIP

ISBN 1 85278 325 7 (cased)
        1 85278 598 5 (paperback)

Printed in Great Britain by
Billing & Sons Ltd, Worcester

Contents

Figures

Preface

This book has a long history and there are many debts which ought to be recorded. Unfortunately history accumulates debts, but it does not make it any easier to remember them and so I must apologize for those I overlook.

There have been teachers who I would like to thank, for instance Richard Sutch who did me the service of teaching macroeconomics from *The General Theory* and Bent Hansen who taught an exciting course on the microfoundations of macroeconomics. There have been many generations of students at UEA who have helped pedagogically and substantively with the argument. Then there are my colleagues at UEA who in one way or another have been concerned with macroeconomics: for instance, David Bailey and Ashok Parikh. Two deserve a special mention: Steve Rankin because I have taught with him on so many macro courses; and Robin Cubitt because he read and provided valuable comments on some of this book.

I wrote most of this book while spending a year at the University of Sydney, teaching on both the economics and political economy programmes. It was a marvellous year (for which thanks go to all my colleagues there). I did much of my writing sitting in the shade of a gum tree, accompanied by two splendid cats Dodgey and Blob who kindly shared their house with us for the year. I benefited from discussions with my macro colleagues at Sydney, Jeff Sheen and Tony Phipps, and I owe a particular debt to Tony Aspromourgos because he read an early draft of the book, and to Flora Gill. In particular, some of the argument in Chapter 6 comes from joint work with Flora.

Finally, there is the publisher. Edward has been encouraging me without success to write a macro text for years. Inadvertently, he recently suggested that I write a microeconomics text. Actually, perhaps he had simply given up all hope of ever getting anything on macroeconomics out of me! Anyway, it might have been this that finally stirred me into action because although this is a book on the microfoundations of macroeconomics, it is unashamedly a book on macroeconomics. In fact, I do not believe that microeconomics can be sensibly undertaken without macrofoundations.

Paradoxically, perhaps, the need for macrofoundations has emerged most clearly in recent times from the literature which has been concerned with the microfoundations of macroeconomics. In fact, I do not think this insight has ever been as clear in the mainstream literature as it is now and I welcome it because it is one reason why macroeconomics is such an exciting area to be working in at the moment. Some may find this an idiosyncratic interpretation of the reviving fortunes of macroeconomics. So be it. What is not in dispute, however, is that there is an enjoyable buzz in macroeconomics these days; and it is this sense of excitement which explains why I wrote this book.

1. An Overview

1.1 Introduction

This is a textbook that draws together the central ideas of the New Keynesian Macroeconomics (NKM) and sets them in dialogue with the New Classical Macroeconomics (NCM). The NKM has been responsible for a significant shift in the analysis of the origins of unemployment and the role of government policy with respect to the macroeconomy. In particular, NKM strengthens the case for activism in demand management as opposed to the hands-off stance favoured by the NCM; and it suggests a new arena for government activism on the supply side of the economy.

The choice of the term New Keynesian Macroeconomics to describe these ideas is somewhat self-conscious and self-serving in the way that it echoes the New Classical Macroeconomics. However, there is more to the choice than mere posturing. The NKM parallels exactly the NCM by making distinctive contributions to the explanation of expectation formation and wage and price determination. In particular, the NKM draws attention to several problems with the hallmark NCM assumptions of rational expectations and competitive market clearing prices.

One theoretical problem, common to both the NCM account of rational expectations and the setting of wages and prices, helps explain the title of this book. This is the difficulty of providing an account of where the beliefs which individuals entertain about the behaviour of other individuals (agents) come from. Hence 'belief and social interdependence' appear in the sub-title, and they are joined by 'time' because the 'problematic' behaviour of others is sometimes bound up with their expectations about the future.

The problem arises in both the field of expectation formation and wage and price setting because there are typically many different beliefs about other individuals which will support self-confirming outcomes. That is to say, there are a number of beliefs which satisfy the condition that when the belief is widely acted upon it produces outcomes which confirm that belief. In these circumstances, beliefs can no longer simply be fixed within the model by appeal to the relevant equilibrium concept because there are multiple equilibria. Instead, the choice of belief involves an additional act of coordination – since any of the candidate beliefs will be confirmed provided others also entertain it, the trick to belief formation is to coordinate your choice with that of others.

This coordination will be achieved when individuals condition their beliefs on the same piece of 'extraneous' information; and one equilibrium will thereby be selected from among the many. By definition, the information used must be extraneous to the model because the model itself generates multiple equilibria, and the act of conditioning on the same piece of extraneous information provides the source of coordination. This use of shared sources of extraneous information is akin to the following of a convention. Consequently, one way of expressing the NKM theoretical criticism is that the NCM slides over the necessary role played by conventions in economic life.

This is a matter of some consequence when we turn to questions of policy. The various potential equilibria have very different welfare properties and so how one equilibrium rather than another comes to be selected can matter deeply. For instance, some mechanisms of belief coordination will yield an equilibrium with unemployment. I shall not be saying very much about how the government might affect economic outcomes by influencing the mechanisms used to coordinate beliefs in the private sector. This is the potential new domain for government supply-side policy, which I referred to in my opening paragraph, and as yet there is little in the literature on this topic. However, the NKM does more on the policy front than single out this new arena for policy to go to work. Their analysis makes a direct impact on the traditional policy debate over demand management activism by showing that it turns in some degree on what mechanisms are in place for coordinating beliefs. In particular, some ways of coordinating beliefs make government demand management policies a potent influence on the welfare characteristics of the equilibrium and others do not.

To conclude this brief introduction, it may be helpful to make these same points slightly differently and more specifically by locating the NKM in the discussion of the microfoundations of macroeconomics. NKM offers a set of imperfectly competitive microfoundations for the supply side of the macroeconomy. This means it is concerned with how agents decide what price to set and output to produce given the level of demand; and the contrast is with the competitive microfoundations found in the NCM where prices and output emerge from the condition of market clearing. The choice of microfoundations is important because it has a major impact on the policy debate. I will state the matter plainly. The case for activism on both the demand and the supply side is strengthened with imperfectly competitive microfoundations. First, it is likely to introduce some nominal price stickiness with the result that nominal demand shocks have long-lasting effects on output (that is, because output deviates significantly from its long run, stable inflation, value). Second, it is likely to introduce some real price stickiness with the result that real shocks, particularly supply shocks, have permanent effects on output (that is, because the long run, stable inflation, value of output changes).

Two possible policy inferences might be drawn from this: either intervene on both the demand and supply side when there are demand and/or supply side shocks; or engineer a competitive supply side to the economy so that such interventions become unnecessary. The NKM argument, however, goes further than this. It tells against the latter because a competitive *laissez-faire* market is not a serious, in the sense of practical, option.

The competitive option seems more mythical than real because the informational base to support such a system seems extremely unlikely. In particular, the NKM reminds us that uncertainty about the future and the impactness of some information undermine the possibility of competitive exchanges and transactions. Since economies that operate in historical time and where there is a significant awareness of social interdependence are bound to suffer from these informational disorders, it seems that the appropriate starting point for policy is an acceptance of some form of imperfect competition. Once this is recognized, a potential activist role for demand management looks more assured and the question with respect to supply-side activism turns on how to influence the behaviour of agents in these markets. This is where the NKM puts conventions (and institutions which embody those conventions) on the agenda of supply-side economics because, in their analysis of imperfect competition, these conventions crucially affect the character of market outcomes.

1.2 A Detailed Outline

I shall indicate in this outline not only what material I cover and how I build the NKM argument but also the generic types of models I shall be introducing to discuss the theory.

I begin with two chapters which set the scene for the later discussion of the NCM and NKM contributions. They are designed to provide a point of continuity between the usual fare of first and second year macroeconomics courses and the more advanced material presented in the remainder of the book. However, it would be disingenuous to claim that they are merely a recap. They are more selective and finely focused than the usual intermediate macro course. In fact, the material has been organized so as to bring out how the unemployment policy debate turns significantly on the choice of microfoundations (or to echo the sub-title, on the way social interdependence is modelled). In particular, that the role for activism on demand and supply sides depends on how expectations are formed and how nominal and real wages and prices are determined. Thus I hope to motivate the later NKM contributions in these areas.

Chapter 2 begins with the so-called neoclassical synthesis and develops this into an aggregate demand/aggregate supply model with competitive microfoundations. Here the aggregate supply relationship is understood in the Friedman/Lucas manner as plotting how the equilibrium output level depends on the relation between prices and price expectations.

Chapter 3 derives a similar aggregate demand/aggregate supply model from imperfectly competitive microfoundations where prices do not clear markets. In particular, prices and wages are not adjusted continuously. Instead they are set for discrete periods according to a normal-cost pricing and a target real wage model and then trades occur at these possibly 'false' (that is, non-Walrasian) prices. The models of 'trading at false prices' are developed here to illustrate how nominal price stickiness can produce a distinctive 'Keynesian' type of unemployment which can be usefully influenced through active demand management.

However, once prices are allowed to change in accordance with normal cost pricing and the target real wage, the model which I derive here looks very similar to the one derived in Chapter 2 using market clearing microfoundations. Indeed, it generates a similar insight with respect to how expectations generating schemes affect the efficacy of active demand management. Notwithstanding this appearance of similarity, there are crucial differences in the matter of how the aggregate supply function is interpreted and this has a further impact on the policy debate. First, the assumption of discrete price-setting introduces some nominal price stickiness which, as noted above, creates scope for beneficial demand management during what otherwise could be a lengthy period of adjustment following a demand shock. Second, the imperfect microfoundations mean that the stable inflation output level is unlikely to enjoy the normative properties of full employment. This recognition is an invitation to supply-side policies based on a better understanding of how imperfectly competitive markets operate.

Chapter 4 puts the NCM through its paces and thereby advances the claims of the competitive microfoundations. It sets out the major arguments of the NCM in detail. First, there is the policy impotence proposition which comes from attaching rational expectations to Chapter 2's competitive market clearing version of the aggregate demand/aggregate supply model. Second, there is the argument that government discretion generates a sub-optimal choice for monetary policy because it introduces a problem of time inconsistency with the optimal policy. This issue is discussed in the context of a game which is played between the government and the private sector. Not unsurprisingly, given the theme in this book of the indeterminacy which arises as a result of interdependence, many of the arguments in the book can be (and are) usefully and succinctly put in game theoretic terms. I assume no special knowledge of game theory here or later. This particular discussion introduces the Nash equilibrium concept.

The latter part of this chapter turns to the NCM models of the business cycle.

I first consider the model of the political business cycle which comes from exploring the time inconsistency issue in the context of a repeated game between the government and the private sector. This is the first substantial piece of game theory in the book and I utilize the perfect equilibrium concept suggested by Selten (1975) and the sequential equilibrium concept developed by Kreps and Wilson (1982a) for the analysis of repeated games. Second, I discuss the various models of the real business cycle which have been generated through real shocks, like productivity surges, changes in tastes, and so on. In particular, I focus the formal discussion on an infinitely lived, representative agent model as this type of model has been central to much of the NCM.

Chapter 5 initiates the discussion of NKM ideas. It focuses on difficulties with the rational expectations hypothesis. Since I wish to separate the issue of rational expectation formation from the matter of whether prices clear markets, all the models in this chapter assume market clearing prices. I start with a simple model of the financial sector to illustrate the difficulties which can arise with respect to learning a rational expectation. This model is easily extended to show the possibility of speculative bubbles and 'sunspots' equilibria. The existence of multiple equilibria poses a new type of learning problem, which can be usefully clarified by thinking of the formation of expectations in a game theoretic context. When there are multiple rational expectations equilibria (Nash equilibria in the expectations game), individuals have to learn not just the structure of the game but also what extraneous information other individuals use to select one from among the many Nash equilibria.

The second half of the chapter works extensively with a simple overlapping generations model. This helps to demonstrate the general properties of the multiple rational expectations equilibria. In particular, how some exhibit cyclical, chaotic, bootstrap, and sunspots behaviour and how the efficacy of demand management can depend on the mechanisms used by the private sector to coordinate beliefs and select an equilibrium.

Chapter 6 develops the NKM explanation of why prices may fail to adjust to nominal demand shocks (that is, it offers a justification for the assumption that prices do not continuously adjust which was used in Chapter 3 and which helped motivate the argument for demand activism). I call this nominal stickiness. Three broad explanations can be distinguished. One is rooted in the connection between nominal and real price stickiness when firms/agents entertain a particular set of what can prove to be rational expectations about the behaviour of others. In particular, a nominal demand shock will be experienced by each firm as a real shock when each firm expects other agents not to adjust. Consequently, the response of each firm will depend on how sensitive its prices are to real shocks – that is, what I call its real price sensitivity. Thus the discussion of nominal stickiness leads me to consider the issue of real stickiness, which it will be recalled (from Chapter 3) also directly affects the argument for supply-side activism. The central NKM insight now is that we might find real price inflexibility when there are small menu costs because the gains from price adjustment are only second order when others are not expected to adjust. Thus, real price stickiness can lead quite rationally to non-price adjustment by all in response to a nominal shock when all expect non-adjustment, and this behaviour then sustains the original expectation of non-adjustment. Typically, this is not the only equilibrium since the individual incentive to adjust rises with the expected degree of adjustment elsewhere and so there is likely to be at least another equilibrium where all expect each other to adjust and each thus decides to adjust, thereby confirming the original expectation of adjustment. Consequently, the issue of equilibrium selection when there are multiple rational expectations equilibria surfaces again (and with it the potential importance of conventions).

The second explanation of nominal price stickiness, like the first, utilizes a model of monopolistic competition and it turns on the properties of staggered price-setting in such a market structure. To motivate this explanation, it is shown how such staggered arrangements might emerge as information-generating devices on the state of nominal demand.

The final explanation of nominal stickiness comes from an understanding that prices are often set to preserve 'trust' in a long-term economic relationship and that such pricing can run counter to the dictates of short-run profit maximization. The importance of 'trust' is explored in a duopoly model where firm interaction takes the form of a repeated prisoner's dilemma game. In particular, it is shown how one conditional/punishment strategy (tit for tat) can be a perfect equilibrium in such a game and how price stickiness might be a feature of this equilibrium.

Chapter 7 completes the discussion of NKM by considering the determination of wages. The structure of the argument connecting nominal with real stickiness is exactly the same as that found in Chapter 6; so is the explanation of nominal stickiness which is run through staggered wage setting. Consequently, this chapter focuses immediately on the sources of real wage stickiness. It begins with a discussion of why labour markets are likely to be imperfectly competitive and then studies the behaviour of wages in several imperfectly competitive models: in a monopoly union model; in a Nash and other bargaining models; and in efficiency wage models. These models span the spectrum of possible wage-setting arrangements from unilateral union determination to joint determination to unilateral firm setting. They yield similar conclusions. Real wage responsiveness is likely to depend on the precise conventions which are employed in labour markets; thus reinforcing the general message on the importance of conventions in economic life. This is particularly clear in the discussion of bargaining models where I offer a critical evaluation of the Nash solution to the bargaining game.

The chapter concludes with a reminder of how real wage stickiness connects with the policy debate. It can contribute to nominal wage and price stickiness and so strengthen the case for demand management activism. In addition, supply shocks will occasion significant output changes when there is real wage stickiness and so such stickiness will motivate supply-side activism.

I hope the overarching theme of 'time, belief and social interdependence' has not been lost in this detailed outline of the NKM argument. In case it has, and as a ready-reference should it get lost again at a later stage, let me finish this outline by reweaving the theme back into the story. 'Time' features significantly in two ways in the material I have just sketched. First, it takes 'time' for information to become available to agents in an economy with the result that they can face a problem of distinguishing nominal from real demand shocks. A system of staggered wage and price setting can evolve as a response to this problem and such arrangements impart inertia to prices and wages in response to nominal demand shocks.

Second, there are multiple rational expectations equilibria in competitive sequence economies, that is in economies which operate in historical as opposed to logical 'time'. This multiplicity poses the question of how one equilibrium is selected. Selection here involves coordinating your beliefs with other agents and this is where 'time' intersects with 'belief' and 'social interdependence'. This connection is crystallized by the existence of conventions: they are devices for selecting an equilibrium and they assume a central importance because the different equilibria have varied welfare properties and can be variously affected through demand management.

Multiple equilibria also arise with respect to wage and price setting, even when 'time' poses no special problems. They occur, so to speak, as a result of pure 'social interdependence' in these instances. Again the selection of an equilibrium depends on agents coordinating their beliefs via conventions or some similar selection device. And again the selection matters deeply because some conventions will deliver both nominal and real wage and price stickiness and these rigidities underpin the claims of demand and supply policy activism respectively.

1.3 The Place of New Keynesian Macroeconomics

I have set the NKM ideas in the context of the standard macroeconomic debates in Chapters 2 and 3 for two reasons. First, as I have already mentioned, this is a textbook and I hope that this scene-setting will make the material available in a manner suitable for courses in macroeconomics. Second, I believe that this contextualization helps to reveal the strange, but nevertheless significant, progress which has been made in macroeconomics since the publication of Keynes's *General Theory*.

To be able to note some progress anywhere is always satisfying, and so I make no excuses for taking the opportunity here! However, it would be disingenuous if I were to leave matters quite like this. This progress is both strange and it goes beyond the debates in macroeconomics over demand management activism, and the like, into some of the central issues in social theory. I shall say a bit more about this now because I do not intend to dwell on it in the text.

First, let me say something about the strange nature of this progress. Economics is fractured into an orthodoxy and its critics; and the latter takes the former seriously in a manner which is rarely reciprocated. This is, perhaps, as it must be given the prerogatives of orthodoxy. I have written this book within the orthodoxy, so to speak, because this has been the *modus operandi* of the NKM. However, I think it should be recorded that there is little in the NKM which has not been well understood, albeit in a different and often less formal manner, in Post Keynesian circles for a very long time. Indeed, one of the hallmarks of the Post Keynesian tradition is the argument that the particular institutional and historical context in which an economy operates critically affects the behaviour of that economy. It has simply taken the orthodoxy rather a long time to come to the same conclusion. There are many interesting questions which might be asked about the method of a discipline which goes in for bouts of 'rediscovery' in this way. But, this is not the place to pursue them. I wish only to record the intellectual debt to Post Keynesianism now because it will go largely unacknowledged in the rest of the book.

To turn to matters beyond economics, the insights of the NKM can be related to some of the central debates in social theory. One concerns the relationship between the individual and society. The liberal view of this relationship suggests that society can be understood, at least in principle, as the interaction between autonomous individuals. Individuals are typically understood for this purpose in a way familiar to economists: they have a set of well-behaved preferences and they are deemed instrumentally rational because they act so as to satisfy best those preferences. Thus society contains no mysteries in the sense that if we start out with a knowledge of the preferences of individuals and assume that they act so as to satisfy those preferences then we can predict what will happen as they interact. Or to put it round the other way, we can always explain what happens in society, albeit with a suitable acknowledgement to the history of previous interactions settling the constraints under which each individual now pursues his or her interest, by reference to the preferences of the individuals who comprise that society now.

This liberal view in social theory is also, despite the usual array of 'ifs', 'buts' and qualifications along the way, unambiguously allied with arguments for a minimal state in political and economic theory. Let me remind you briefly of the connections here. In liberal political theory the state is understood as a contract that arises between individuals who realize that the pursuit of their interests may be best served on certain matters by making and implementing decisions collectively. Orthodox neoclassical economic theory, in turn, supplies the insight that competitive markets supported by well-defined property rights deliver (pareto) efficient outcomes, and consequently we might expect individuals, in an ideal world at least, to contract for a state which only ensures the institutional prerequisites for competitive markets and well-defined property rights.

Of course, Keynes took issue with the orthodox theory of his time, what he referred to as Classical economics. He doubted that the free play of market forces would generate efficient outcomes. Market forces could not guarantee the full employment of an economy's resources and the state would have to assume a more active role with respect to the economy. Keynes's argument here might be construed as simply a concern with a contingently contested claim about the behaviour of the economy. However, what the NKM has helped to reveal is that a basis for Keynes's arguments can be found in a necessary reconceptual-ization of liberal notion of the relation between the individual and society.

It is the NKM emphasis on the possibility of multiple equilibria and the necessity of individuals using pure coordinating devices which recasts the liberal notion of the relation between the individual and society. The social is always more than the sum of its individual parts in NKM because the shared rules of thumb (the conventions) which coordinate individual behaviour are irreducible. They cannot be reduced to and explained in terms of the preferences of individuals and their presumed instrumental rationality. In this way, the NKM provides ammunition for those critics, especially in sociology and anthropology, of liberal political theory.

In other words, the NKM makes the argument of Keynes more theoretically substantial than is sometimes imagined; and in so doing it is connecting the insights of Keynes to some of the central arguments in social theory. Or to put this in yet another way, the rush to provide microfoundations for macroeconomics can be seen in this context as the conscience of liberal theory at work in economics. The contrasting claim of the NKM that there are irreducibly social elements in individual behaviour cashes in as a call for macrofoundations of microeconomics and this echoes the thoughts of many critics of liberal theory.

1.4 A Final Disclaimer

I make no claim to originality in the presentation of the theory in this book. All the models are 'borrowed' from somewhere. This is as one might expect in a textbook. I hope only to have ordered the material in a revealing way. Where the models are generally known in the literature through their association with a particular author, as for instance in the case of Friedman's natural rate hypothesis, I have explicitly credited the author in the text. Otherwise, I have kept such references in the text down to a minimum. I have preferred, instead, to give a brief guide to the literature at the end of each chapter. This guide centres on what I take to be the crucial contributions. Of course, it reflects my own reading and so I am bound to have overlooked some important contributions. All I can do is offer a blanket apology in advance to those authors that I have failed to include and to my readers.

There is one general reference that I should give at the outset. It applies to almost every chapter and I shall not note it again. This is Blanchard and Fischer (1989). This book came out after I had started this text, but it covers much of the ground and it has been a very useful reference. It is much more comprehensive in its discussion of the literature than this book is. By comparison, my book is a dash through the literature, touching only those bases which are necessary to keep the argument over policy up and running. I can warmly recommend Blanchard and Fischer to anyone who wishes to follow some part of my argument in more detail through the labyrinth of the wider literature.

I have deliberately kept the models simple where possible and I have blended diagrammatic explanations with those running through simple mathematics. Plainly, simplification comes at some cost in terms of generality. But, I have not simplified in any area where I believe that more complicated models yield qualitatively different results.

It only remains for me to record a belief that I think it has been a long time since macroeconomics has been as exciting as it is now.

1.5 Brief Notes on the Literature

The term NKM has been used now in a number of survey articles to describe certain ideas over expectation, price and wage formation: for instance, Ball, Mankiw and Romer (1988), Rotemberg (1987) and Gordon (1990). It should be noted that the usage is not without difficulty because there is a book by Frank (1986) which uses the title *New Keynesian Economics* to describe rather different insights.

The Post Keynesian tradition is heterogeneous. But its origins are to be found in the work of Joan Robinson and Michel Kalecki and it runs through the work of Robert Eichner, Paul Kregel, Paul Davidson, Hyman Minsky and many others. The connections between Keynes's work and the issues in political theory which I note (and with philosophy more generally) have recently been brought to the fore by the contributions of Carabelli (1988), Fitzgibbons (1988) and O'Donnell (1989). There is one other person who ought to be mentioned in this area, although neither NKM nor the Post Keynesians seem especially keen to recognize him, and this is Leijonhufvud (1968).

Giddens (1979) and Douglas (1982) are good sources for sociological and anthropological criticisms of the foundations of liberal theory, and I have a book, Hargreaves Heap (1989) which explores some of the issues in the relation between economics and liberal theory. There is a large literature on the microfoundations of macroeconomics (see, for instance, Phelps, 1970) and Foster (1987) is a recent counter which emphasizes the irreducibility of some macro behaviour.

PART 1

The Background

2. The Neoclassical Synthesis and the Natural Rate Hypothesis

2.1 Introduction

This chapter and the next provide the background for the debate between the New Classicals and New Keynesians. In many respects they describe the state and terms of the debate between Keynesians and their critics as it was up until the early 1970s. But to say only that these chapters furnish a historical backdrop is misleading. They are more important than this. The models in both chapters supply the influential building blocks for those later positions and they establish the lines of the contemporary argument over both demand management and supply-side policies.

In particular, the accommodation between Keynes and the Classics that is offered by the neoclassical synthesis provides an understanding of the proximate origins of unemployment which feeds directly into the NCM and *laissez-faire* supply-side economics. The hallmark of this understanding is that unemployment results from an inappropriate real wage.

Neoclassical synthetic models combine the Keynesian theory of aggregate demand with the (neo)classical theory of aggregate supply and I begin this chapter with a typical, early version. It has unemployment arising because nominal wage rigidity prevents the adjustment of the real wage to its equilibrium value. In these circumstances, demand management becomes an alternative way of achieving the equilibrium real wage by altering the general level of prices. The policy debate within this framework is sketched in section 2.3: it turns on the relative efficacy of such demand manipulations as contrasted with a reliance on the emergence in due time of some flexibility in the nominal wage.

The weakness in these early models was the presumption of nominal wage rigidity. Friedman (1968) and Lucas (1973) remedy this weakness whilst preserving the connection between unemployment and the real wage. They are the direct links from this tradition to the NCM. They argue that real wages (and more generally relative prices) are set at the inappropriate level because of mistaken price expectations. In sections 2.4 and 2.5 I present Friedman's model and the associated twist in the policy debate. Nominal wages always move to clear the market but because of mistaken price expectations the market clearing wage is not the Walrasian one. In these circumstances, the policy debate turns on whether demand manipulations aid or hinder accurate expectation formation; and the stage is set for the NCM.

Section 2.6 formalizes the discussion of the 'modern' neoclassical synthesis by developing a log linear model which combines Keynesian aggregate demand theory with Friedman/Lucas aggregate supply analysis. I conclude the chapter with some brief notes on the literature.

2.2 The Basic Model

The following assumptions characterize a typical model in this tradition, and they also serve to introduce the notation.

1. There are three physical commodities: capital (K), labour (L), a single final commodity (Y) which can be used either for consumption (C) or investment (I); and two financial assets, money (M) and bonds (B).
2. Firms are profit maximizers.
3. Firms operate everywhere 'as if' they were in competitive markets and thus are price takers and accept the price for final commodities (P), the wage rate for labour (W) and the interest rate (r).
4. Each firm has an identical production function exhibiting constant returns to scale and diminishing marginal returns to each factor $(Y=f(K,L);$ $f_L > 0,\ f_{LL} < 0)$.
5. The capital stock is fixed in the short run for firms.
6. The supply of labour depends positively on the real wage.
7. The demand for consumer goods is a function of disposable income and wealth.
8. The demand for investment goods depends on the expectations of future levels of demand for final outputs and real interest rates.
9. The demand for money depends on income, wealth, interest rates and expected future interest rates; and bond demand is wealth minus money demand.
10. The government can tax (T), purchase the final commodity (G), and it can control the money supply and issue government bonds.
11. All expectations of future variables are held constant unless otherwise stated.
12. Financial markets clear through movements in r.
13. Final commodity markets clear through movements in P.
14. The money wage is fixed until full employment, at which point it moves to clear the market.

The penultimate section contains a log-linear representation of this model.

This is a mathematically convenient way of representing the model for some of the later discussions. But, for now, it is quite sufficient to discuss the model qualitatively with the aid of some diagrams.

The assumptions 2 to 5 generate two important relationships: the aggregate supply function, and the aggregate demand for labour function. Under competitive conditions the demand for labour is generated by equating the real wage with the marginal physical product of labour. Thus each firm's demand for labour (as a function of the real wage) coincides with the marginal physical product of labour function; and with the usual 'well behaved' production function, this will be a decreasing function of the level of employment. The same relationship will be preserved in the aggregate as we sum across all firms to derive the market demand for labour, and this is plotted in the fourth quadrant of Figure 2.1 where the labour market is depicted. The third quadrant contains the aggregate production function and is a vehicle for translating the aggregate level of employment from the fourth quadrant into the amount of output supplied in the second quadrant.

Assumptions 7 to 12 are essentially those which generate the standard IS/LM representation of a closed economy. I will say something more specifically about open economies later in this chapter and in other chapters. For now, I have chosen a closed economy for convenience. It reduces the number of assumptions without losing all generality, since one could always specify an open economy where the exchange rate moves to maintain purchasing power parity and where there is imperfect capital mobility and the IS/LM part of the model would behave in exactly the same way as the closed economy counterpart. By itself and for a given P, the IS/LM model is usually understood as determining the level of output. In the context of this larger model, where there are explicit supply-side decisions and the price level is free to move, the model is treated as determining the relationship between aggregate demand for final output and the price level. This aggregate demand relationship is plotted in the second quadrant. For a given fiscal and monetary policy stance, aggregate demand rises as prices fall because, in the IS/LM, a fall in prices produces an increase in real money balances which raises aggregate demand initially through lowering interest rates and priming investment. Of course, the connections between price changes and aggregate demand can be more complicated than this. But nothing is gained at this stage by opening-up that complexity: suffice with the thought that any wealth effects are of second order significance and can be ignored; and the economy is not operating anywhere near a liquidity trap or an interest insensitive portion of the investment demand function. Finally, it should be noted that changes in monetary and fiscal policy stance will, in these conditions, also unambiguously shift the function out for expansionary changes and vice versa.

In Figure 2.1, the first quadrant contains a purely technical device. It plots

Figure 2.1 Neoclassical synthetic model

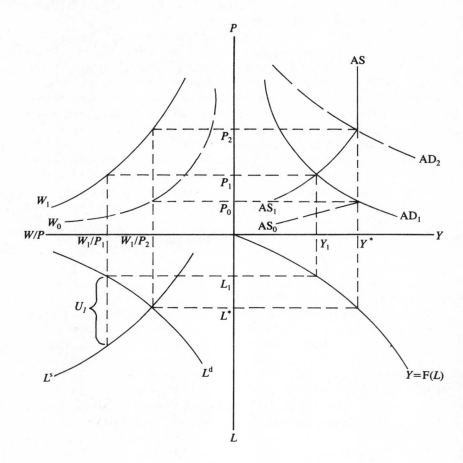

the relationship between the real wage and the price level for a given money wage (*W*) and it serves to capture the force of the assumption 14.

Assumption 6 is responsible for the supply of labour function in the third quadrant. It can be derived from the utility maximizing behaviour of individuals, but there is nothing special about this since a variety of other behavioural postulates are also consistent with such a function.

Finally, assumption 13 is used to determine prices in the second quadrant, where final commodity markets are depicted.

Thus, in summary, the heart of these assumptions and the subsequent analysis is contained in the second and fourth quadrants, where the final commodity and labour markets are depicted. The other two quadrants contain purely technical devices for relating the analysis of each market to the other.

What, then, has happened to the remaining commodities and financial assets noted in assumption 1? In effect, assumption 5 means there is no market for existing capital goods because firms are stuck with whatever capital stock they have inherited from history; and the money market and the bond market are behind the scenes. The operation of the money market has been taken into account in the construction of the aggregate demand function in the second quadrant; and we have ignored the bond market altogether, courtesy of Walras's law.

That completes the tour of how these assumptions have been crystallized in this diagram. Let us now see what insights on unemployment can be generated by the model.

2.3 First Observations on the Unemployment Debate

I begin by constructing the aggregate supply function. Take some price level, say P_1; we see from the first quadrant that this fixes the real wage at W_1/P_1. We now follow this wage down to the labour market and find that firms employ L_1 units of labour, and from the third quadrant, we know this means that Y_1 units of output will be produced in the final commodity market. Repeated application of this analysis for different price levels yields the aggregate supply function which has been depicted in the second quadrant. One word of further explanation is in order. It will be remembered that assumption 14 has money wages moving to clear the labour market once full employment has been reached. Thus for any price above P_2, we can note that at the fixed money wage W_1, there would be excess demand for labour and consequently the money wage would not remain fixed. It would be bid up until the real wage which equates labour demand with labour supply is reached, with a corresponding equilibrium level of employment at L_2 yielding output equal to Y_2. In this model, L_2 and Y_2 are the full employment levels of employment and output and hereafter will be denoted by L^* and Y^*.

To illustrate the potential for unemployment in such a model, let us suppose that aggregate demand occupies the location given by AD_1. The equilibrium level of output would be Y_1 since P_1 is the price which clears final commodity markets and this generates a real wage W_1/P_1 leading to employment of L_1. The labour market does not clear here: L^s exceeds L^d and unemployment equal to U_1 has emerged.

Thus under these conditions, our model generates an equilibrium characterized by unemployment. In addition, the geometry of the diagram makes plain that, in principle, there are two ways in which an equilibrium where the labour market clears might be achieved. One is for the aggregate demand function to be shifted out to a location like AD_2. This would push the price level up to P_2 and in turn this would lower the real wage to the market clearing value (W_1/P_2). Such a movement in the aggregate demand function could be achieved through an expansionary change in monetary and/or fiscal policy.

Alternatively, if the money wage were to fall in response to the unemployment, then the aggregate supply function would start to move out as each price level would now be associated with a lower real wage and consequently firms would decide to employ more labour and supply more output at each price level. Indeed, when the money wage falls to W_0 in the diagram and the aggregate supply function shifts to AS_0, there will be full employment with a price level P_0 and a real wage which is the same as W_1/P_2.

Thus we have the debate in a nutshell: either governments can intervene with a judicious manipulation of aggregate demand, or market forces can be relied on eventually to bring about the necessary adjustment of the real wage. Which should be preferred? This seems to depend on the contingencies of the actual economy. If, for instance, money wages, as a matter of fact, are sticky and respond only sluggishly to the excess supply in the labour market, then it is expedient to manipulate demand. From a purely theoretical perspective, there appears to be no reason for preferring one to the other.

2.4   Mistaken Expectations and the 'Modern' Aggregate Supply Function

In the context of the 1960s when nominal wages in most OECD countries demonstrated great flexibility, at least in an upward direction, it became difficult to maintain an analysis of unemployment which turned on significant wage stickiness (assumption 14). Friedman (1968) provides one way of introducing wage flexibility into the model without altering any of the other basic elements. The model suitably amended is capable of generating employment variations and it preserves the essential insight of the early models that employment variation arises because of movements in the real wage.

You will notice a slight but significant change in terminology. I have not referred to unemployment here, rather it is to employment variations. It may seem that this is no more than a semantic quibble since, when employment moves below the full employment value, one is inclined to imagine unemployment is the result. And, indeed, in a deep sense this is correct. Nevertheless, the choice of phrasing also signals an important difference in Friedman's analysis. He has nominal wages always moving so as to clear the labour market; and so there is never 'unemployment' in his model in the sense of excess supply. The trick as far as employment variation is concerned is that the equilibration need not occur at the Walrasian full employment value. In particular, the behaviour of participants in labour markets when setting the money wage is motivated by the real wage rate and so depends on expectations about the general level of prices. Accordingly, when these expectations are wrong the market can equilibrate at a different level of employment. However, notwithstanding this difference, the deeper sense in which it still makes sense to talk about Friedman's analysis as being concerned with unemployment is that the non-Walrasian employment levels are not pareto efficient; and most people worry about unemployment in the conventional sense of excess labour supply because of similar welfare losses. In fact, the only difference is that in the one case unemployment is visible and in the other it is disguised.

To tease out Friedman's result on employment variation (disguised unemployment), I shall make the following alternative assumptions to 14. These assumptions are captured in Figure 2.2 which focuses on the labour market.

14a. The money wage moves to equilibrate the labour market.
15. Workers decide how much labour to supply at each money wage by forming an expectation of the price level, thereby translating the money wage into its real wage equivalent, and it is the expected real wage that determines how much labour is supplied, as in assumption 6.
16. Employers decide how much labour to demand at each money wage by using their knowledge of the general level of prices to translate the money wage into its real wage equivalent, which is then equated with the marginal physical product of labour for profit maximization as in assumptions 2 to 5.

In Figure 2.2, there are a family of labour demand and supply curves, each supply curve is based on a different expected level of prices (P^e) and each demand curve is based on a different actual level of prices. Every family member bears a distinct relationship to each other because each has been derived from the same labour supply or demand function in Figure 2.1. They only differ according to the assumed level or expected level of prices. Thus, to illustrate the point, W_0 when prices are expected to be P_0^e yields the same labour supply, L^*, as the money wage W_1 when prices are expected to be P_2^e, since both money wages translate with these different price expectations into the same expected real wage.

One word is in order before we explore the implications of this way of determining the money wage in the model. Why have I assumed that workers must form price expectations while employers know the price level? There are a variety of ways in which this, or its equivalent, might be justified. I offer the following rationale (the Lucas model in section 2.6 in effect, offers a different but complementary explanation).

Of course, the assumption of a single final commodity in assumption 1 is unrealistic. It is useful because it keeps things simple. But, it should not blind us to an important difference which emerges between employers and workers

Figure 2.2 Competitive labour market equilibrium

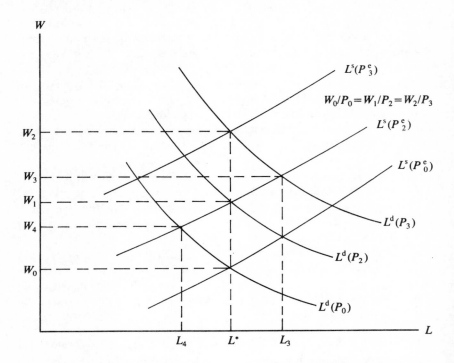

in the real world when there are a variety of commodities. Workers, when they decide how much labour to supply, are concerned with what the money wage will buy in terms of a bundle of goods. In contrast, employers only care about the real wage in terms of the commodity that the workers will be producing. The price of other goods does not affect the firm's decision of how much labour to employ in the production of a particular good when it can only produce that good. Now, while it is plausible to assume that employers know the price of the good which they are engaged in producing, it is less likely that workers know the prices for all the commodities which enter into their wage bundles. Accordingly, the workers' supply decision will depend on price expectations while firm demand for labour depends on actual prices.

Figure 2.3 plots the aggregate supply functions associated with this model of the labour market. To illustrate this derivation, consider a particular level of price expectations, say P_2^e. When $P = P_2^e = P_2$, then the operative labour demand and supply functions are given by $L^d(P_2)$ and $L^s(P_2^e)$, and so the labour market will clear with the wage rate at W_1 and employment at L^*, yielding output equal to Y^*. However, when $P = P_0$ and we have the same

Figure 2.3 Aggregate supply

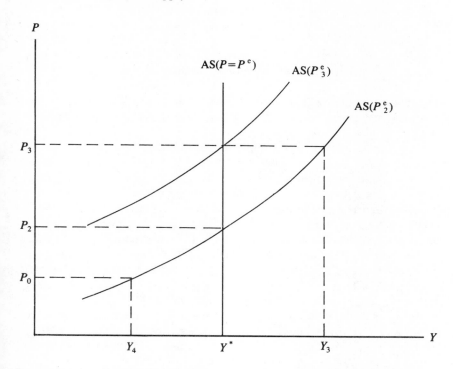

price expectation, the operative labour demand function becomes L^d (P_0) and the operative labour supply function remains L^s (P_2^e). Now, when the money wage moves to clear the market, it will take the value W_4 and the employment level will be L_4, yielding output equal to Y_4. In a similar vein, when $P=P_3$ and the same price is expected, the operative labour demand becomes L^d (P_3), and the labour supply function remains the same and so the wage moves to W_3 with employment L_3 and output at Y_3.

The same analysis can be repeated for any level of price expectations to derive the other members of this family of aggregate supply functions. Finally, it will also be noted that whenever prices are the same as price expectations the labour market always equilibrates at L^*, with output at the full employment value Y^*. Hence I have drawn in a vertical aggregate supply function under these circumstances.

2.5 Second Observations on the Unemployment Debate

Disguised unemployment is possible with this model of the labour market and it arises for the same reason as the model in the second section in this chapter. For instance, in the case we have just considered when price expectations are P_2^e and prices are at P_0 and there is employment at L_4 it is the real wage which is too high because the money wage at W_4 is too high. It should be at W_0, when prices are at P_0, to generate labour demand of L^*. The only difference with respect to the analysis concerns our understanding of why money wages and real wages take on the 'wrong' values. They are set too high because workers expect a price level above the one which actually obtains. Market forces go to work, it is just that they are guided in the wrong direction because of expectational errors.

What is the role for government demand management policy in these circumstances? The answer to this depends on how demand management might affect the occurrence of expectational mistakes; and Friedman's short general answer is that errors are more likely to occur when the government is actively managing demand in a Keynesian fashion than when it adopts a 'hands-off' stance because government activism simply adds to the climate of instability and uncertainty which makes the formation of accurate expectations so difficult.

The longer answer involves a theory of how individuals form their expectations. Friedman (1968) uses a model of adaptive expectations. Under this scheme, individuals adjust their expectations in the light of the errors they have experienced with their previous expectations. Thus in equation 2.1, expectations of the future price in time period $t + 1$ are revised upwards or downwards from the expectation of the previous period t depending on whether the last period's expectation proved to be an under or overestimate, where λ is the coefficient of adjustment.

$$P^e_{t+1} = P^e_t + \lambda(P^e_t - P_t) \qquad (2.1)$$

To bring out the policy implications of nesting this particular expectational assumption in the model, I shall consider a sudden shift in aggregate demand from AD_2 to AD_1 in Figure 2.4 – due, say, to a disturbance in the private sector. This shift causes a fall in output with unchanged price expectations to Y_4, and a fall in prices to P_4. Under the adaptive scheme, price expectations track experience and so this fall in prices will also initiate a revision of price expectations because prices (P_4) no longer match price expectations (P^e_3). This revision will continue until price expectations are again consonant with experienced prices. The geometry of Figure 2.4 suggests that this will occur when prices and price expectations equal P_2 – any other expected price and, given AD_2, the actual price will diverge from this expectation thus provoking a revision in price expectations. Once prices and price expectations converge on P_2, full employment is restored. Thus, by nesting the adaptive expectations hypothesis in the model, there is a mechanism which guarantees the restoration

Figure 2.4 Aggregate demand and aggregate supply

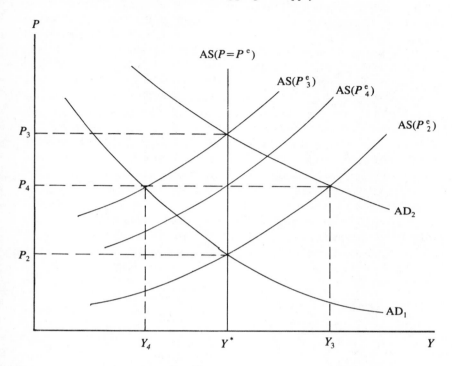

of full employment after a buffeting to aggregate demand. There is no need for government intervention to secure full employment.

Nevertheless, should the government rely on this mechanism? Or should it forestall the whole process through a judicious manipulation of fiscal and/or monetary policy so as to restore aggregate demand to its original location at AD_2? The answer to this question would seem to depend on the relative speeds of adjustment of expectations and the government to shocks of this kind. If expectations are slow to adjust, then the case for government intervention looks strong. Alternatively, if expectations adjust relatively quickly and governments suffer from recognition and execution lags, then the case for a 'hands-off' approach is strengthened.

Of course, the form of this policy argument turns on the assumption of this particular expectations generating mechanism. The adaptive scheme may seem reasonable at first sight, but it does have a peculiar property. When prices rise and there is a gradual process of adjustment of price expectations up to the new higher level and during this period of adjustment, individuals always make the same kind of error. Individuals always underestimate the actual price level. Just how gradually price expectations adjust and how persistent is the error of underestimation will depend on the value of λ. But, unless it is close to 1, the period of adjustment will be significantly greater than a single period.

This peculiarity is one reason why later theorists have preferred the rational expectations hypothesis. We shall pursue this later, for now it is perhaps worth noting that this peculiarity was also the source of Friedman's explanation of the inflationary consequences of Keynesianism. To appreciate the point, consider a shift of the aggregate demand schedule now from an original position of AD_1 to AD_2 in Figure 2.4. Governments, guided by Keynesian arguments with respect to demand management, would always be tempted to make such a change because in the short run, before price expectations had fully adjusted, there would be a boost to output and employment. It would seem that during the period when price expectations are below the actual price level, as for instance initially in Figure 2.4 when P_2 continues to be expected despite the rise in price to P_4, Keynesian results have been produced by the expansion in demand: output and employment have expanded. However, Friedman was quick to point out that this was only a temporary, short-run effect that arose during the period it took for price expectations to be revised fully in line with experience. In the long run, once these revisions have been made, it is easy to see from Figure 2.4 that since price expectations which coincide with experience ($P=P^e$) produce the vertical aggregate supply function for the economy, the only effect of the increase in aggregate demand is to raise prices from P_2 to P_3.

Naturally, whether this observation is really a telling complaint within this framework against such expansionism will depend on how long the 'long run' is here. Is it, for instance, the kind of 'long run' in which we are all dead? This is the kernel of Keynes's general doubts about policies which look alright in the long run, and one wonders whether it might apply here. But to answer this question is, of course, to answer the same question that we encountered a moment ago in the discussion of judicious manipulations of demand to iron out private sector disturbances to aggregate demand. Both turn on the issue of how quickly price expectations adjust to experience.

2.6   A Log-linear Version of Aggregate Demand (IS/LM) and Aggregate Supply (Friedman/Lucas)

This section offers a simple log-linear version of the AD/AS neoclassical synthetic model. Lower case for a variable denotes the log of that variable, except for 'r' which stands for the interest rate, and a subscript index of t, $t + 1$, etc. refers to the time period. In general I shall either use greek symbols for parameters or lower case letters subscripted by numbers (this practice should help distinguish the parameters from the log of variables).

I shall begin with aggregate supply and I will offer two derivations. The first follows Friedman (1968), as sketched in Figure 2.4. The aggregate production function is Cobb-Douglas with a fixed capital stock and is given by

$$Y = \alpha L^\beta \tag{2.2}$$

Profit maximization under competitive conditions yields the standard first order condition from which we derive labour demand,

$$W/P = \alpha\beta L^{\beta-1} \tag{2.3}$$

Labour supply is given by

$$L^s = (W/P^e)^\gamma \tag{2.4}$$

Taking logs and setting labour demand equal to supply, equilibrium (log of) employment and output are

$$l = \gamma[\log(\alpha\beta)+p-p^e]/[1-\gamma(\beta-1)] \tag{2.5}$$

$$y = \log(\alpha) + \gamma[\log(\alpha\beta)+p-p^e]/[1-\gamma(\beta-1)] \tag{2.6}$$

Defining y^* as the log of output when the labour market clears with price expectations which are confirmed, then 2.6 has the form, for any period t, of

$$y_t = y^* + a_0(p_t-p_t^e) \tag{2.7}$$

Lucas's 1973 model uses what is often referred to as the 'islands' approach – the terminology is from Phelps's (1970) original discussion. Imagine many geographically scattered competitive markets producing the same good. Each market is served by worker-producer firms; and these firms respond to perceived relative price changes between the price of the good (p_i) in their market i and the general price level (p). Firms must form an expectation with respect to the general level of prices and so an industry supply function takes the form

$$y_i = \mu + \phi[p_i - E(p)] \tag{2.8}$$

Each market suffers from two types of shock: one is specific to that market and affects p_i; and the other is part of a general nominal shock to all markets and affects both p and p_i. Equation 2.8 implies that each firm only wishes to respond in real terms to the sector specific shocks. These sector specific shocks sum to zero across all markets because they represent redistributions of demand between markets. So, each firm knows that

$$p_i = p + z \tag{2.9}$$

where $z \sim N(0, \text{var}(z))$. Before observing p_i, each firm believes that, because there are nominal shocks, p is drawn from a population with $E(p)$ and a $\text{Var}(p)$. The task of the firm then becomes to update this expectation of p once p_i is observed so that a supply decision can be made in accordance with 2.8. Utilizing 2.9, the firm can generate a least squares projection for p and this is given by

$$E(p|p_i) = (1-\theta)E(p) + \theta p_i \tag{2.10}$$

where $\theta = \text{var}(p)/[\text{var}(p) + \text{var}(z)]$. This will make some intuitive sense because it implies that as $\text{var}(z)$ gets smaller and smaller, given 2.9, p_i becomes a better and better indicator of p. Once 2.10 is substituted into 2.8 and we sum across all industries, the aggregate supply (y) function becomes

$$y = \Sigma\mu + \phi\theta[p - E(p)]. \tag{2.11}$$

In short, we obtain an expression of the form given by 2.7.

To complete this representation of the economy, I turn to aggregate demand. Assumptions 7, 8 and 10 are represented by

$$\begin{aligned}
C_t &= c(Y_t, A_t, T_t) \\
I_t &= i(r_t, p^e_{t+1} - p^e_t, Y^e_{t+i}) \\
G_t &= G_t
\end{aligned} \tag{2.12}$$

The goods market equilibrium condition implies

$$Y = c(..) + i(..) + G$$

This implicitly defines the IS curve and I shall approximate the explicit solution to this with the following log-linear relation

$$y_t = b_0[r - (p^e_{t+1} - p^e_t)] + b_1 g_t + b_2 \tag{2.13}$$

where b_0, b_1 and b_2 are parameters which capture the influence of wealth, the expected future levels of output, for constant expectations, and the specifics of the consumption and investment functions; g is an index of fiscal policy stance.

Assumption 9 is represented by

$$(M/P)^d_t = m(Y_t, r_t, r^e_{t+i}, A_t) \tag{2.14}$$

With constant expectations, I approximate this by a log-linear relation and by substituting this into the equilibrium condition for money markets, I obtain the LM curve given by,

$$m_t - p_t = c_0 y_t + c_1 r_t + c_2 \qquad (2.15)$$

The substitution of 2.15 into 2.13 yields the following aggregate demand function

$$y_t = [b_0(m_t - p_t + c_2)/c_1 - b_0(p^e_{t+1} - p^e_t) + b_1 g_t + b_2]/(1 + b_0 c_0/c_1) \quad (2.16)$$

This establishes a particular model where there is an inverse relation between prices and demand and where the location of the aggregate demand function depends on, amongst other things, the fiscal and monetary stance of the government. These were features which I utilized in the construction and discussion of Figure 2.4. Likewise, equation 2.7 provides a particular model where the aggregate supply function takes the general form which I have assumed in Figure 2.4. Not unsurprisingly, by combining 2.7 and 2.16, I derive the earlier conclusion that while monetary and fiscal policy changes can influence aggregate demand, they will only affect output when they produce a gap between prices and their expected values.

2.7 Brief Notes on the Literature

Hicks (1937) introduced the IS/LM representation of aggregate demand and Patinkin (1965) is usually credited with providing the earliest, complete version of a neoclassical synthesis. I have already mentioned that Friedman (1968), Phelps (1970) and Lucas (1973) are the central references behind the reinterpretation of the aggregate supply function.

I have focused on the policy debate with respect to activism versus 'hands-off', but there has been another important aspect to the policy debate, which I have not touched upon because it has receded in importance. Nevertheless, I should perhaps say a little bit about it now because in one way or another it has been important in developing our understanding of the determinants of aggregate demand. It was (and still is) concerned with the relative efficacy of monetary as contrasted with fiscal policy as a tool for manipulating aggregate demand. There were many strands to this aspect of the debate involving different theories of consumption, investment, and so on (see, for instance, Friedman (1957)) and it has its new twists and turns (for instance, Barro (1974) on fiscal policy and Laidler (1984) on the so-called 'buffer stock' approach to monetary policy). There were also important further developments with respect to the analysis of aggregate demand in open economies. Initially, for instance, there was Meade (1951) and Mundell (1963). The latter introduced the concept of perfect capital mobility and this makes the relative efficacy of monetary and fiscal policies depend critically on the exchange rate regime of the country.

There have been several further developments on the open economy theme, some of which are more appropriately acknowledged later as they belong more closely to the debates between NKM and NCM. However, there is one which should be mentioned now: the 'small open economy' assumption. This is associated not only with the assumption of perfect capital mobility, but also with the assumption of a world price for tradeable goods (see Johnson (1976)). In a simple model, where all the economy's goods are tradeable, this means that under fixed exchange rates the price level is given to the economy by that which prevails on world markets. Consequently, an increase in aggregate demand does not produce a rise in prices. Instead, it causes excess demand which is satisfied by sucking in more imported goods. Thus changes in demand only affect the external trade account.

3. Trading at False Prices, Imperfect Competition and NAIRU

3.1 Introduction

This chapter develops models where agents trade with each other at fixed 'false' prices – 'false' prices are non-Walrasian equilibrium prices. To appreciate the potential relevance of these models, it may be helpful to think of an economy without the information-generating device of the Walrasian auctioneer. In the absence of an auctioneer or some such, it must be firms and individuals who set prices and if they do not continuously adjust prices but rather set them for discrete periods of time, then the phenomenon of false trading will arise whenever those agents fail initially to set Walrasian prices. This makes an interest in the phenomenon of false trading depend on significant nominal wage and price rigidities, but this is not obviously unrealistic. Most actual markets do not seem to operate with continuous prices setting. Instead, prices and wages do seem to be set for significant periods before they are reset and I shall be discussing some of the reasons behind this nominal rigidity in Chapters 6 and 7.

These models are important because they suggest another proximate cause of unemployment. Unemployment can arise not only, as it does in the neoclassical synthesis, because real wages are too high, but also because there is an inadequate level of final demand in relation to the general level of prices and money wages. In short, the problem can lie with nominal wages and prices in relation to nominal demand and not just with real wages. When unemployment arises from this new 'nominal' source, it is sometimes referred to as 'Keynesian' unemployment while the real wage variety is designated 'Classical'. I shall use this terminology from now on.

The recognition of another sort of unemployment crucially opens up the policy debate. To be specific, when unemployment is 'Keynesian', the case for activism on both the demand and the supply side of the economy is strengthened – and this conclusion still stands once we allow for the periodic adjustment of wages and prices.

Let me explain in more detail how I develop the argument to support this conclusion. I begin with a simple model of false trading in the next section. It follows the original Barro and Grossman (1971) contribution in this field and illustrates the possibility of Keynesian unemployment. This is generalized in the following section to allow for trades at any vector of false prices. Some false prices generate 'Keynesian' non-Walrasian equilibria, but others produce non-Walrasian equilibria where unemployment is associated with an inappropriate real wage. Thus the phenomenon of false trading does not preclude 'Classical' unemployment, but it does alert us to the possibility of an additional variety of unemployment, a 'Keynesian' sort.

The occurrence of 'false' prices may not cause surprise, since there is no auctioneer in the real economies. Nevertheless, it stretches credulity to work with permanently fixed prices. Firms and individuals do adjust prices and wages even if only at discrete points in time. Consequently, the fourth section introduces some wage and price dynamics into the model of false trading. In particular, I append a normal cost pricing hypothesis and a target wage model to a case of Keynesian unemployment. These particular dynamics have two plausible claims to our attention in this instance. First, the phenomenon of false trading is intimately bound up with the failure of the conditions of Walrasian competitive equilibrium to be satisfied. So, it is natural to look to models, like these, of wage and price setting under conditions of imperfect competition. Second, these dynamics are commonly used in the applied macroeconomics literature for OECD countries.

However, the use of these imperfectly competitive wage and price dynamics has a strange effect. It produces a model which is in many respects formally identical to the Friedman (1968) version of the neoclassical synthesis that I discussed in sections 2.4 and 2.6 of the previous chapter. In other words, it seems that there is a formal agreement between the neoclassical synthesis of the last chapter and the imperfectly competitive inspired models of this chapter.

Plus ça change, rien ça change, it seems! The formal similarity, however, is deceptive. There are important differences of interpretation which have a significant affect on the policy debate; and I draw these out in section 3.5. In particular, I conclude that the case for policy activism is strongest in the model with imperfectly competitive microfoundations. Thus the choice of microfoundations for macroeconomic theory has a critical impact on the policy debate.

3.2 Keynesian unemployment

The following assumptions will be made to illustrate the possibility of unemployment that is unrelated to the level of the real wage.

1. There are three commodities: capital, labour, and a final commodity; and one financial asset, money.
2. Firms are profit maximizers.

3. Firms operate as price takers and so accept the price for final commodities and the wage rate for labour.
4. Each firm has an identical production function exhibiting constant returns to scale and diminishing marginal returns to each factor.
5. The capital stock is fixed in the short run.

These assumptions are, to all intents and purposes, identical to those in the synthetic model of Chapter 2. There is a difference in the interpretation of assumption 3, of why firms are price takers. It is no longer because they operate in Walrasian competitive markets. Instead they accept the price because they have set it and will not change it during the period which we shall be analysing (see assumption 8 below). The only real analytic difference is a simplification which has come through paring the financial assets down to one, money.

6. The supply of labour and the demand for final commodities depend on the utility maximizing decisions of individuals who have well-behaved utility functions (that is, individual i: $U_i = U(Y_i, 24 - L_i^s, M_i)$; $U_j > 0$, $U_{jj} < 0$ for $j = Y, 24 - L^s, M$).
7. The government can control the money supply.

In effect, assumptions 6 and 7 here cover the same ground as 6 to 10 in the synthetic model. This model is more compact because neoclassical, optimizing microfoundations have been used rather than the IS/LM model to generate the demand and supply functions for commodities, and because the government's role is restricted and there is only a single financial asset.

8. The wage and price vector $[W,P]$ is given exogenously.

This assumption covers the ground of 12 to 14 in the synthetic model and reflects the switch from a world where prices move to clear markets to one where nominal prices and wages are set for discrete periods of time and need not clear markets (Chapters 6 and 7 explore the foundations for such an assumption in detail). Finally, we need make no assumption regarding expectations here since the model has no explicit dynamic features when individuals perform these one period-like utility maximizing calculations.

The formal representation of assumptions 1 to 4 for a typical firm is given by

$$\text{max: } P.Y - W.L^d$$

$$s.t \ Y = F(L) \tag{3.1}$$

Likewise, we have the typical individual's behaviour in 6 represented by

$$\max: \ U = U(Y^d, 24 - L^s, M^d)$$

$$s.t \ P.Y^d + M^d = W.L^s + \pi + M^s \tag{3.2}$$

where π is the individual's share in profits.

For convenience I have dropped the subscript i when referring to a particular individual or firm. Firms are already identical by assumption and I extend this now to individuals as nothing is gained in this instance by having individuals who are different. Thus, I obtain the expositional simplification that market behaviour is simply the typical individual's or firm's behaviour writ large.

Figure 3.1   Competitive equilibrium in the goods and labour markets

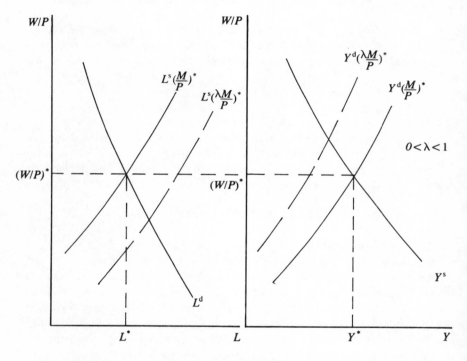

The solution to 3.1 yields the conventional downward sloping demand for labour and the upward sloping output supply functions in Figure 3.1; while 3.2 generates the output demand and labour supply functions. These latter functions depend on the real value of initial money holdings (M/P) since this helps, along with the real wage rate, to locate the budget constraint. I have drawn a pair of dotted functions in this figure, based on a lower real value of initial money holdings. Lower initial money holdings increase the amount of labour supplied at each wage and lower the amount of final output which is demanded because I assume that both leisure and the final commodity are normal goods and so the demand for both drops as wealth falls.

The original position of these functions produces a simultaneous equilibrium in both markets with the real wage equal to $(W/P)^*$. This defines the Walrasian equilibrium: it is a pair $[W.P]$ such that their ratio $= (W/P)^*$ and such that their absolute level makes the initial nominal money supply equal to $(M/P)^*$ in real terms.

Now, let us suppose this equilibirum is disturbed by a fall in the nominal money supply (to λM) with unchanged prices. The functions shift to their dotted locations and both markets are thrown into a state of excess supply at the Walrasian equilibrium real wage. Classical economists would, then, have argued that this places downward pressure on money wages and prices which will continue until the fall in prices restores the real value of the money supply to $(M/P)^*$. Once this is achieved, L^s and Y^d regain their original location and the equilibrium in both markets is restored, with the real wage unchanged. This follows directly from the standard inference that these functions are homogeneous of degree zero in $[W,P,M]$ – in other words, that individuals do not suffer from money illusion. Thus, an equiproportionate change in W,P and M will leave demand and supplies unchanged, and preserve $(W/P)^*$ as the equilibrium real wage. Hence, nothing changes on the real side of the economy as a result of the nominal shock once wages and prices have adjusted.

This seems a straightforward argument and it implies that re-equilibrating forces will be set in train the moment a nominal disturbance of this sort occurs. But it glides over a potential difficulty: what happens if individuals and firms trade before these price adjustments have been made? To focus on this possibility, I assume that wages and prices have been set for some time period and so remain initially at their old values – that is to say, the real wage is at its Walrasian equilibrium value, the problem is simply that the nominal level of wages and prices are too high relative to the new, lower nominal money stock.

When trades occur at the old vector of wages and prices, individuals encounter a constraint in the labour market because they are not able to sell all the labour they would like. Likewise, firms encounter a constraint in the final commodity market as they are unable to sell all that they would like. These constraints need to be taken into account in the utility maximizing and profit maximizing decisions portrayed in equations 3.1 and 3.2, and they will alter the behaviours of both firms and individuals.

Let me deal with the phenomena of quantity constrained maximization generally by first taking an illustrative set of demand constraints. I shall suppose that when supply exceeds demand in a market, the shortfall in demand is allocated equally by some mechanism across all firms/individuals in that market. Thus I assume that, for a set of demand constraints, a typical firm encounters final demand $=Y_1(<Y^s)$ and a typical individual encounters demand for labour $=L_1(<L^s)$. Accordingly, firms have an additional constraint:

$$Y=Y_1 \tag{3.3}$$

And the new budget constraint for individuals is

$$P.Y^{d'} + M^{d'} = W.L_1 + \pi' + M \tag{3.4}$$

In recognition of the additional constraints in 3.4, I have indicated with a superfix dash that the demand for commodities and money will change. These are the effective demands, the actual demands which individuals will make once they take account of the constraints they have encountered in the labour market. They can be contrasted with their notional and unconstrained counterparts which come from 3.1 and 3.2. In particular, since $L_1<L^s$ and since $Y_1<Y^s$ implies actual profits (π') are less than notional profits (π), it follows that the right-hand side of the constraint in 3.4 has been tightened as compared with 3.2; and so the effective demands which satisfy 3.4 must be less than their notional counterparts in 3.2. I plot just such an effective demand for final commodities in Figure 3.2. It lies inside the notional demand at the Walrasian real wage for the reason I have just sketched. It will also coincide with the notional demand curve at some lower real wage because a lower real wage would eventually reduce labour supply sufficiently to remove the constraint in the labour market. Finally, I have drawn it as vertical when it departs from the notional function because I assume that there is no redistribution effect on demand as the share of income between profits and wages is altered. In practice, a redistribution is likely to have two conflicting effects: a fall in the wage share is likely to lower consumption, but in a dynamic setting the rising profit share might boost investment by raising profit expectations. So, it is, perhaps, not unreasonable to assume that such changes in the real wage produce no net effect on aggregate demand.

Similarly, once equation 3.3 is recognized by firms, their notional demand for labour is superceded by an effective demand. Firms face a particular level of demand for final output, they would like to produce more at the current real wage, but as there is no final demand beyond Y_1, they decide to produce Y_1 and this alters their demand for labour. An example of their effective demand is given by $L^{d'}$ in Figure 3.2. Again it is drawn for a given constrained level of demand in final commodity markets and so long as this constraint is binding this will generate a unique level of demand for labour which can be obtained through evaluating the inverse of the production function

Figure 3.2 Trading at false prices: notional excess supplies

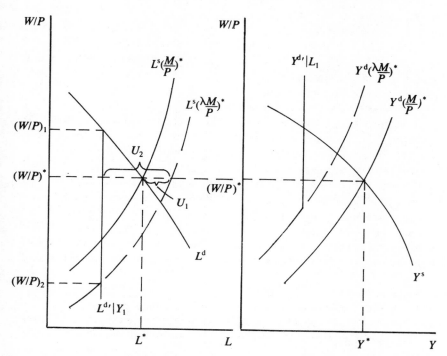

at this level of output ($N^{d'} = F^{-1}(Y_1)$). The vertical portion of the effective demand function is rather special in the sense that it depends on there being a single variable factor of production and the absence of a redistribution effect upon aggregate demand. The latter means firms always have to employ a certain amount of labour to produce the constrained level of output, and the former means that the constraint does not vary with changes in the real wage, which is what we have assumed earlier in the construction of $Y^{d'}$. Strictly speaking, it is also worth pointing out that had we worked with an open economy then we would have had further to assume a constant effective exchange rate since a fall in the real wage that was occasioned by a devaluation of the exchange would prime the demand for output. Anyway, to complete the derivation, at some point with rises in the real wage, the constraint in the final commodity market ceases to be binding and thereafter the effective demand for labour coincides with the notional at some higher real wage.

These curves have been drawn for some unspecified set of demand constraints. For a non-Walrasian equilibrium to obtain, the effective demand for labour in the aggregate must be such that it is based on an effective level of final demand which would emanate from individuals encountering that level of constrained employment. Thus, as I have drawn it in Figure 3.2, we would have a non-Walrasian equilibrium only if $Y^{d'} = Y_1$ and $L^{d'} = L_1$. In general, such an equilibrium will emerge once a Walrasian equilibrium has been disturbed, provided the usual properties for macroeconomic equilibrium are satisfied – like a marginal propensity to spend out of income which is less than one. But it will not be generated instantaneously. Instead, one can follow any disturbance through a figure like 3.2 and one will observe a multiplier process whereby lower output lowers employment which in turn lowers final demand and output, leading to lower employment and yet lower final demand and so on. Several things are noteworthy about this non-Walrasian equilibrium. Two have a particular relevance for the themes of this book.

First, unemployment occurs even though the real wage is at the Walrasian equilibrium value. This is plain from the diagram, and even if the real wage fell to equilibrate effective labour demand with supply, there would still be underemployment (disguised unemployment) because the economy would not be operating at the Walrasian level of employment. In effect, a fall in the real wage here does not increase employment, it merely serves to transfer workers from the unemployment line into a state of 'leisure' via a discouraged worker effect.

It is important to note that although the 'no increase in employment' result is rather special, since it depends on the vertical portion of the effective demand for labour function, the proposition about underemployment remains quite general. In particular, the effective demand for labour function will not coincide with the notional demand for labour function even when, for the reasons set out above, the effective function is sensitive to the real wage throughout. Consequently, even when the real wage moves to equate effective labour demand with labour supply and this leads to increases in employment because the effective demand for labour is sensitive to the real wage, the level of employment thus achieved will still be below Walrasian equilibrium level of employment. In short, there is an aspect to the unemployment problem here which has nothing to do with an inappropriate real wage – a distinctly Keynesian aspect which arises because nominal wages and prices fail to adjust.

Second, unlike the price adjustment process imagined by Classicals, the quantity adjustment scheme which I have sketched actually exacerbates the original disequilibrium. Witness Figure 3.2, where the unemployment in labour markets expands from U_1 to U_2 as quantity adjustments take place.

A couple of further observations, while not central to the argument, are worth making in passing. First, the marginal productivity theory of wage determination will only hold as a special case in such a non-Walrasian equilibrium. To see this we can return to Figure 3.2. A variety of real wages are consistent with the level of employment set by $L^{d'}$: any wage between

$(W/P)_1$ and $(W/P)_2$ and the demand for labour will be the same. But only one, $(W/P)_1$, will be equal to the marginal physical product of labour at that level of employment since it is only at this wage rate that the economy would also be operating on the notional demand for labour function where the 'marginal productivity = real wage', profit maximizing condition holds. Thus, in general, one might expect the real wage to be below the marginal physical product of labour.

Second, the process of incorporating the quantity constraint into the individual's utility maximizing plans provides a possible justification for the conventional treatment of the consumption function in the macroliterature. The point to be remembered here is that the usual macroconsumption function can not just be an aggregation of conventional individual demand functions. Conventional demand functions are functions of the vector of all prices. They do not contain composite price and quantity variables like 'labour income' because the supply of labour is endogenous to the utility maximizing decision. Consequently, the presence of such an argument in the macroconsumption function is likely to appear somewhat puzzling from a conventional theoretical point of view – even *ad hoc*! However, once it is acknowledged that individuals may encounter a quantity constraint in labour markets, then the income variable becomes immediately explicable as a recognition that utility maximization has been additionally quantity constrained.

To conclude this section, we have a model of trading at false prices where unemployment is not caused by real wages being too high. Instead it is the nominal level of wages and prices in relation to the level of nominal demand which is the cause of the problem. In a world troubled by this problem, an increase in aggregate demand can prime employment because it relaxes the constraint faced by firms in product markets: a boost to final demand feeds through to increase the effective demand for labour and employment rises without any change in the real wage.

3.3 A Generalization of Trading at False Prices

It may be tempting after the discussion in the last section to dismiss Classical unemployment. After all, there is no auctioneer in the real world to call out the price vector *à la* Walras and prices do seem to be set for discrete periods of time, so it would be pure serendipity if the economy happened to go to work with anything that approximated the Walrasian price vector. However, this dismissal would be a mistake. Many of the insights of the previous chapter with respect to Classical unemployment are not undermined by the phenomena of trading at false prices.

To appreciate the potential continuing relevance of the models in Chapter 2, I need to do two things. One is generalize the model of the previous section, which I shall do now. The other is introduce some wage and price dynamics – this I do in the next section. The generalization is necessary because I used a special sort of non-Walrasian price vector in the last section: one which generates constraints for suppliers in both markets. In principle, it seems possible that other non-Walrasian price vectors could produce any of a variety of constraint configurations across the two markets; and the non-Walrasian equilibria associated with these other vectors may well exhibit the property of 'Classical' unemployment. Indeed, this is exactly what happens.

We have three further possible constraint configurations to consider: demanders constrained in both; demanders in final goods markets while suppliers are constrained in labour markets; and vice versa. To map these possibilities and see what price vectors are associated with what constraint configurations, I shall consider another specific case of trading at false prices: one where the real money supply is above the Walrasian equilibrium value ($=\mu M$ where $\mu > 1$). It is depicted in Figure 3.3.

Figure 3.3   Trading at false prices: notional excess demands

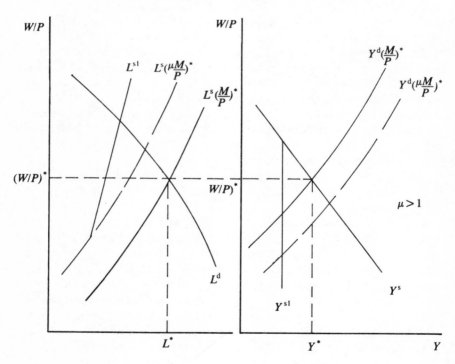

On this occasion, both markets suffer from excess demand and it is the demanders who are constrained. As before, these constraints force firms and individuals to reappraise their notional decisions and I have drawn in the results: $L^{s'}$ and $Y^{s'}$. The intuition behind the particular shapes for these effective supply functions is something like this. There is no point in offering to supply labour when you cannot obtain goods with the wages which are thereby gained. So, the effective supply of labour function is drawn inside the notional counterpart at $(W/P)^*$. At some lower real wage the effective function will coincide with its notional counterpart because a lower real wage would eventually remove the constraint in final commodity markets. Finally, the function is drawn with some positive sensitivity to the real wage because I assume that individuals do not believe that they will be constrained forever. So they become willing to supply more labour at higher real wages now, even though they cannot purchase more goods now, because they think they will be able to purchase goods at some future date. In short, this sensitivity reflects an intertemporal substitution of leisure as the current real wage changes.

Likewise firms, unable to purchase all the labour they would like, are forced to produce output below what they would notionally like to supply. At some higher real wage the constraint in labour markets would be removed and so the effective supply function coincides with its notional counterpart after that point. But, at wages below that value, there is only a certain amount of labour available and so only a certain amount of output can be supplied to final commodity markets.

This case is the exact opposite to the one considered in section 3.2, where suppliers were constrained in both markets, and the two combine to enable the division of the wage and price vector space into the various types of constraint configuration. This is performed in Figure 3.4 and requires some explanation.

For a given nominal supply of money, every wage and price vector can be mapped on to a point in the real wage and real money supply space in Figure 3.4. For example, the Walrasian equilibrium wage and price vector is given by the pair $[(W/P)^*, (M/P)^*]$ in this space.

We know from the analysis in the previous section that a lower real money supply will shoot the economy into a non-Walrasian equilibrium where suppliers are constrained in both markets. To delineate the general boundaries of this regime, we can refer back to Figure 3.2 and note the following. At lower real wages effective demand for labour can be equilibrated with notional supply of labour; and below this rate the labour market will switch to demanders being constrained. Thus combinations of lower real wages and lower real money supplies will preserve equilibrium in the labour market. Hence the ray which shoots out from the $[(W/P)^*, (M/P)^*]$ in the south-westerly direction in Figure 3.4. Likewise combinations of higher real wages and lower real supplies

Figure 3.4 Walrasian and non-Walrasian equilibria

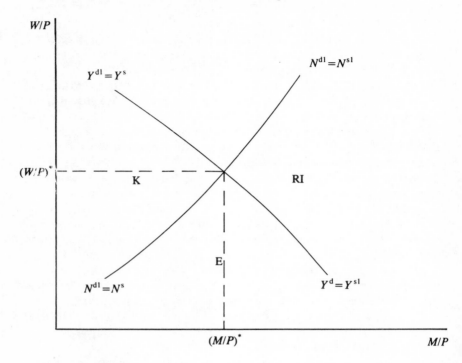

of money can preserve equilibrium in the final commodity market. Accordingly, the region where suppliers are constrained in both markets is given by the fan labelled K (for Keynesian).

A similar consideration of what happens when the real supply of money increases yields the fan labelled RI. To appreciate its derivation, remember that we know from the earlier discussion that the higher real supply of money propells the economy into a non-Walrasian equilibrium characterized by demanders being constrained in both markets, and hence the title RI standing for repressed inflation. Further, we know from Figure 3.3 that higher real wages combined with this higher real supply of money would equilibrate the effective supply of labour with demand; and that lower real wages combined with this higher real supply of money would equilibrate final commodity markets.

The nature of the CL region which lies between these two fans can be determined by reference to those fans. We know from Figure 3.2 that final commodity markets have demanders constrained to the right of the boundary between K and CL. Similarly, we know from Figure 3.3 that it will be the suppliers of labour who are constrained to the left of the boundary between

CL and RI. Consequently, CL corresponds to the configuration where suppliers are constrained in labour markets and demanders are constrained in product markets.

The E region, standing for empty, is the remaining constraint combination with demanders constrained in the labour market and suppliers constrained in the product market. In fact, although this appears to be a discrete region, a moment's reflection suggests that two boundaries $N^{d'}=N^s$ and $Y^d=Y^{s'}$ must coincide, making the E region empty. Firms cannot be simultaneously constrained in commodity and the labour market since only one can be binding at any one time: either it must be the amount of labour supplied which constrains output or it is the level of final demand; it cannot be both unless they coincide. Figure 3.5 amends 3.4 to take this into account.

Figure 3.5   Walrasian and non-Walrasian equilibria

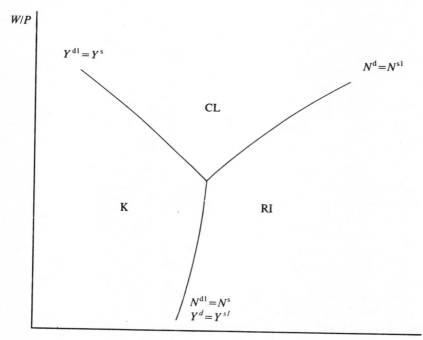

As far as the argument in this book is concerned, it is the CL region which is of interest because it is characterized by unemployment which is significantly different from the 'Keynesian' variety. A typical CL non-Walrasian equilibrium is pictured in Figure 3.6 to bring this out. Unlike the Keynesian unemployment

Figure 3.6   Classical unemployment

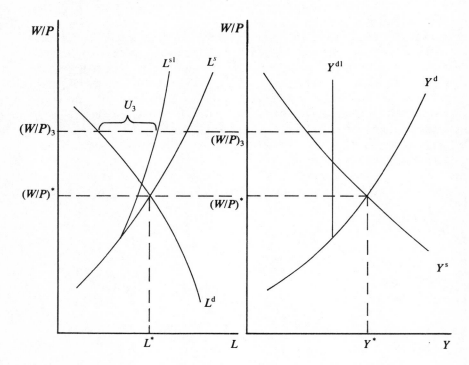

equilibrium, an increase in final commodity demand does not help here. It merely adds to the state of excess demand in final commodity markets. The only way that employment will be primed is through a fall in the real wage.

To conclude this section, trading at false prices can produce a variety of non-Walrasian equilibria. In particular, in this simple model, there are two which are characterized by unemployment. One conforms to the Classical analysis in the sense that real wage adjustments are required for increases in employment. This is the essence of the neoclassical-synthetic view, and so in that sense it offers us no new insights with respect to unemployment than were already available to us in the previous chapter. Nevertheless, it serves to increase the generality of that analysis.

Actually, the neoclassical-synthetic view can now be seen as a special case of Classical unemployment. By relaxing the fixed-price assumption for final commodities, the neoclassical-synthetic model permits these markets always to clear and this corresponds to the boundary line between Keynesian and Classical regions in Figure 3.5. Aggregate demand policies become effective here only because they raise final commodity prices and thereby lower the real wage. This is the key to increasing employment on this boundary since an increase aggregate demand unaccompanied by a fall in the real wage would simply shoot the economy unambiguously into the Classical region, it would add excess demand to final commodity markets and unemployment would be unaffected.

In contrast, the second type of unemployment in this model is wholly new compared with the models of Chapter 2 and provides a different reason for the use of aggregate demand policies as weapons against unemployment. Increases in aggregate demand will raise employment without an adjustment to the real wage because firms are demand constrained in final commodity markets.

3.4 Wage and Price Dynamics

It is useful to work with a fixed wage and price assumption because wages and prices are often set for significant periods of time. However, it can hardly be the last word. Wages and prices may be sticky in the real world, but they are not permanently fixed. Consequently, I need to extend the analysis of the previous section to allow for nominal wage and price adjustments.

However, I shall only do this for the case of Keynesian unemployment. We have already explored in the previous chapter how Classical unemployment can arise when we assume market clearing wage and price dynamics and allow for incorrect expectations (or for some nominal wage stickiness). So, there is not much to be gained by looking at the Classical case again now.

The question, then, is: what wage and price dynamics should we introduce into a Keynesian world? We could use the competitive market clearing wage and price dynamics from the last chapter and simply assume that wages and prices respond to excess demand/supply. But this is not the most obvious choice once we have acknowledged the possibility of trading at false prices due to the absence of the Walrasian auctioneer. It is more natural to think of individual agents setting prices themselves when there is no auctioneer; and this points us in the direction of models of imperfect competition.

Indeed, a moment's reflection reinforces this connection. When we consider the situation in each market after false trading has occurred, it scarcely corresponds to a competitive market even if there are a large number of traders. In particular, neither workers nor firms perceive, as they would in a competitive equilibrium, that they can sell as much as they like at the current wage/price. Instead, workers and firms find themselves in a situation which corresponds much more closely to one of imperfect competition where demand is constrained and where the advantage from changing wage/price will depend on what other participants in the market are expected to do. As Arrow (1959) observed rather famously a long time ago: 'in any situation where supply does not equal demand, it follows the economy will show evidence of monopoly and monopsony' (p.48). In other words, when markets are not in competitive equilibrium, it is models of imperfect competition which will provide the insights into what happens, even though there may be very many traders on both sides of the market.

I discuss a variety of models of wage and price-setting under imperfect competition in Chapters 6 and 7. They both help to explain why nominal wages and prices may not adjust instantaneously to a nominal shock, thus giving rise to false prices, and they give specific insights into how wages and prices might evolve once employment and output have changed as a result of trading at false prices. For now, I consider only two simple imperfectly competitive wage and price-setting mechanisms which capture roughly the analysis of those later chapters. To keep the discussion moving, I will only offer a brief intuitive justification for these mechanisms now, leaving the fuller explanation to later.

Price-setting is covered by

$$P = \mu W \tag{3.5}$$

where μ depends on trend levels of labour productivity, the size of the mark-up and the trend relative price of raw materials.

This is a 'normal cost' pricing hypothesis. It commands reasonable empirical support and as a consequence it is frequently used in applied work on OECD countries, and it makes some theoretical sense from a satisficing, rule-of-thumb perspective whenever the costs of acquiring information over what is the optimal price to charge are significant.

Wage setting is captured by

$$(W/P)_{\text{Target}} = \lambda Y^{\psi} \tag{3.6}$$

$$W = (W/P)_{\text{Target}} \cdot P^{e} \tag{3.7}$$

This is a target wage model where a crucial determinant of the target wage is the level of output in relation to the full employment level. This is not inconsistent with a market forces view of what determines wages when the target is designed to achieve full employment. However, it is also frequently derived from a bargaining model of wage determination, where the target wage varies with level of unemployment because this influences the relative power of workers and employers in the bargaining process.

The substitution of 3.5 and 3.6 into 3.7 yields, after taking logs,

$$p = \log(\mu\lambda) + \psi y + p^{e} \tag{3.8}$$

In effect, prices vary with output and price expectations because the former affects the target real wage and the latter influences how this wage is translated into a money wage, and the money wage feeds into prices because it determines, *ceteris paribus*, the level of 'normal costs'. But notice, equation 3.8 is formally the same as equation 2.6. With rearrangement it could be described in the same way as equation 2.7,

$$y = y^* + a_0 \, (p - p^e)$$

Thus we have derived a formally equivalent description of the economy to the neoclassical synthetic one by combining the model of Keynesian unemployment with these wage and price dynamics. In short, we have two alternative microfoundations for the derivation of the same sort of aggregate supply relationship pictured earlier in Figures 2.3 and 2.4.

There are, however, two important differences. First, the normative attributes of the output level (y^*) generated when price expectations are confirmed are very different. With Friedman, this output is the level which 'would be ground out by the Walrasian system': it is the full employment level of output. With wage and price-setting following equations 3.5 to 3.8, it has no such connotation. Only in the case where the target wage is set to achieve full employment is this so. More generally, in the bargaining version of these functions, it is simply the level of output which generates a level of unemployment such that the balance of forces in wage bargaining establish claims which are consistent with the size of the pie. Accordingly, it is sometimes known as NAIRU (the non-accelerating inflation rate of unemployment) rather than the more emotively charged 'natural' rate.

As an aside on this point, it is perhaps worth noting that NAIRU can be given a slightly different interpretation in an open economy with fixed exchange rates. In this context, μ will depend on the real exchange rate because this will influence the trend relative price of all imported inputs. In addition, the real exchange rate will influence the expected price in equation 3.7. To be specific, let me distinguish between domestic prices P^d and prices on foreign goods P^f, then 3.5 becomes

$$P^d = \mu W \tag{3.9}$$

and 3.7 becomes

$$W = \lambda Y^\phi \, [\alpha P^d + (1 - \alpha) P^f]^{\,e} \tag{3.10}$$

where α is the share of worker's consumption on domestic goods. I can rearrange 3.9 and 3.10 so as to produce expressions for the real wage in terms of domestic goods (W/P^d) and I have plotted them in Figure 3.7 for a given

Figure 3.7 NAIRU

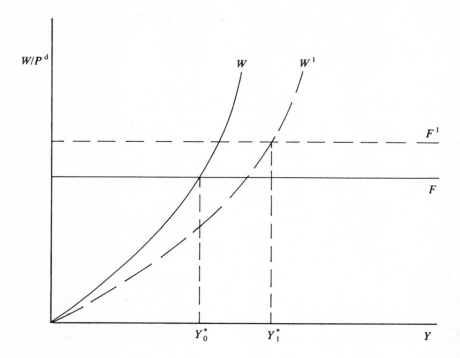

ratio of foreign to domestic prices. Equation 3.9 gives the real wage consistent with the profit expectations of firms (F) and 3.10 gives the real wage which is consistent with the worker's target (W). NAIRU is given by the intersection of the two curves: it is the level of output which reconciles the profit expectations with wage expectations. Now, suppose that the real exchange rate (e) rises. P^f/P^d falls and μ rises (because the relative price of imported raw materials falls): with the result that both W and F shift out to produce a lower NAIRU (higher Y^*). The intuition is simple. A rise in the exchange rate increases real income in the country and this enables workers to enjoy a higher real wage without this conflicting with the profit expectations of firms; and the higher wage is consistent with lower unemployment.

This might seem to imply that the government can choose any NAIRU level it likes through a suitable choice of the real exchange rate. However, there are typically constraints on this choice. In particular, the need for equilibrium in the external account is liable to impose a constraint. Suppose, for instance, the external account is dominated in the long run by the need to maintain current account balance. Then, given the tendency for higher output levels and real exchange rates to suck in more imports, there will typically be an inverse locus of output and exchange rate combinations which yield current account equilibrium. I have drawn this in Figure 3.8 (as BP) along with the positive locus implied by the earlier consideration of how e affects NAIRU. From this, we can see that there is a unique NAIRU and exchange rate which is consistent with equilibrium in the current account and the reconciliation of conflicting claims on the pie.

Figure 3.8 NAIRU and the exchange rate

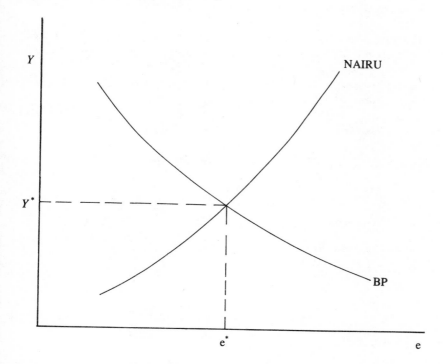

The second important difference between the two versions of the AS functions concerns the direction of causation between prices and output. In Friedman, it is prices in relation to price expectations which determines output because output depends on the real wage. Whereas in the Keynesian aggregate supply function, output is determined by aggregate demand and it is output which fixes prices via the process sketched in equations 3.5 to 3.8. This is not an insignificant difference because it relates back to the distinction between Keynesian and Classical unemployment. When prices deviate from price expectations the real wage deviates from its Walrasian value and this causes

employment to wander from the full employment value in Friedman's natural
rate model. In contrast, when unemployment is Keynesian, employment
changes through movements in aggregate demand and what happens to real
wages with these movements in output depends on the precise specification
of wage and price dynamics. Under those in equations 3.5 to 3.8, the real
wage does not change as output varies.

Both differences in the AS functions have important implications for the
policy debate and I turn to these next.

3.5 A Preliminary Summing-up on the Unemployment Policy Debate

There are three crucial strands to the debate over unemployment which can
now be set out. To focus on these elements in turn, consider Figure 3.9. The
constellation of aggregate supply fucntions can stand for either the Keynesian/
normal-cost/target-wage derivation or the Friedman-like neoclassical synthetic
derivation (even though the understanding of what is implied by Y^* will be
different). The aggregate demand function is in situation AD_1 and I shall
assume that price expectations are P_2^e. Both models predict output will be at

Figure 3.9   Aggregate demand and aggregate supply

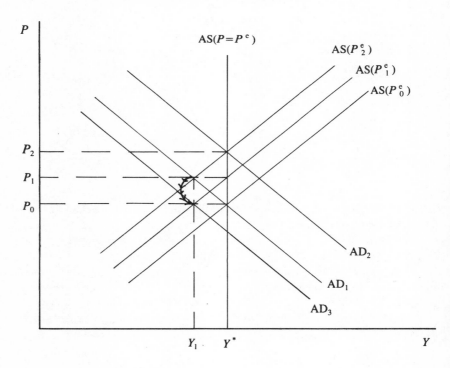

Y_1, below the Y^* level, and there is an unemployment problem. What should governments do, if anything, in these circumstances?

The non-interventionist side of the debate relies on the inference that this is only a temporary resting spot for the economy. Whichever way the aggregate supply function has been derived, price expectations cannot remain at the current value because they are not confirmed by experience. Eventually, prices and price expectations must coincide and when they do the Y^* output level will be restored. The first strand in the debate follows directly from this observation.

It is concerned with the relative speeds of adjustment of price expectations and policy. Will prices and price expectations adjust more or less quickly than the time it takes governments to alter aggregate demand? We have already come across this strand of the argument in section 2.5 and so there is no need to explain again why these variables are important in the debate. I shall be considering what determines the speeds of expectational and wage and price adjustment in the next four chapters and we shall see that significant sluggishness is made more likely when there are imperfectly competitive microfoundations.

The second argument in the debate concerns in more detail the adjustment path under non-interventionism. It is assumed implicitly in the first argument that the crucial determinant of the adjustment path is the speed of wage, price and expectational change. The geometry of Figure 3.7 encourages this view because it is plain that prices and price expectations must fall and that there is encouragement for them to fall with the discrepancy between prices and price expectations at Y_1. Thus, the path of adjustment appears straightforward: it is from P_2^e to P_0^e; and prices must change from P_1 to P_0. These look like simple straightline adjustments and so the only interesting question relates to the speed with which the path is covered; and this depends only on how quickly wages, prices and expectations change.

Nevertheless, the path of adjustment can be more complicated and it is one of the traditional interventionist arguments that this greater complexity provides grounds for preferring the judicious manipulation of aggregate demand. The potential for greater complexity arises because the aggregate demand function can also slip in towards the origin as the economy adjusts to changed price expectations. The source of this change is the expectation of falling prices itself – see section 2.6, where the dependence of aggregate demand on price expectations is made explicit. Keynes himself saw this as a potential danger. He argued that the very fall in prices might encourage people to delay their consumption in the expectation of further price falls. In addition, the expectation of falling prices forces a wedge between the nominal and the real interest rates with the result that the real rate is now higher at each nominal rate than before. Consequently, there will be lower levels of investment at each nominal rate than before. Both arguments point to a slippage in the aggregate demand function.

The geometry of Figure 3.9 makes clear that when downward movements in both the AD and the AS functions follow the revision of price expectations, it is possible for output to fall below Y_1 and P may overshoot the final equilibrium price of P_0. Plainly, the risks of this happening depend crucially on the magnitudes of the expectation effects on aggregate demand. In particular, in Figure 3.9, AD would have to shift further than the location AD_3, as price expectations were adjusted in light of experience to P_2^e, to produce this result. But, in addition, and perhaps less obviously, the likelihood of unnecessary output adjustments increases when the original unemployment is Keynesian rather than Classical.

To appreciate this let us suppose first that the unemployment at Y_1 is Classical in origin and that it has arisen, as in the Friedman story, because expectations are incorrect. There is no inflexibility of wages or prices here: markets have cleared at the wrong price vector simply because of incorrect price expectations. Under these conditions, the outcomes for output and prices are always given by the intersection of the appropriate AD and AS functions.

In comparison, when the unemployment at Y_1 is Keynesian, the adjustment of prices and output to a shift in AD may be quite crab-like before it reaches the point of intersection between the appropriate AD and AS curves. With Keynesian unemployment, output moves in response to aggregate demand because prices are initially fixed and it is only once output has changed, and with it unemployment, that price adjustments commence under the specification in equations 3.5 to 3.8. Accordingly, depending on the relative speeds of adjustment it is possible for output to fall below Y_1 in the course of adjusting eventually to Y^*.

To bring out this difference, consider in Figure 3.9 the case where AD moves to AD_3 as price expectations are revised to P_1^e. With Friedman's account of the matter, output remains at Y_1 until there is a further revision in expectations. However, things are rather different in the case of Keynesian unemployment. At Y_1 once the lower price expectations feed through into lower money wage demands, prices will start to fall, as is suggested by the $AS(P_1^e)$ function. But, given the general presumption of sticky prices, which is necessary for the generation of 'Keynesian' unemployment, this change is unlikely to occur instantaneously. Instead, at $[P_1, Y_1]$, the contraction in demand will be felt directly and output will start to fall in response. It is only later that prices will begin to adjust downwards under the dual influence of lower output and lower price expectations. Consequently, the path of adjustment to $[P_0, Y_1]$ is likely to be circuitous in the fashion suggested by the arrows in Figure 3.9; and it will involve temporary but further reductions in output.

The force of these additional worries about the adjustment path plainly depend critically on the possibility of sticky price adjustments because it is these which produce the Keynesian unemployment with the burden of adjustment to changes in aggregate demand then falling on quantities. This helps to explain again why sticky prices have been at the centre of New Keynesian research.

Thus we have another reason why, despite the formal similarity between the derivation of the aggregate supply function for Keynesian and Classical movements in output, it matters whether the unemployment is 'Keynesian' or Classical. When the unemployment is Keynesian the adjustment path to Y^* is likely to be more circuitous than when the unemployment is Classical. Or to put this slightly differently: we have another reason, as far as the policy debate is concerned, for being interested in the issue of how wages and prices are formed – in the microfoundations of macroeconomics.

(In this context, it is interesting to pursue briefly a further question. Can we say anything about the relative likelihood of Keynesian as opposed to Classical unemployment? Plainly part of the answer to this question will depend on what microfoundations we assume and so whether we introduce significant nominal wage and price stickiness. But, granted some stickiness, part of the answer will also turn on the type of shock. To see this, let us return to Figure 3.5. Suppose the economy starts at the Walrasian equilibrium. A deflationary shock, like a contraction in the money supply, will push the economy into Keynesian unemployment when nominal wages and prices are sticky. Equally, a contraction in investment demand which did not lower the Walrasian equilibrium real wage would have a similar effect. In contrast, a real shock, like a surge in the real wage, will push the economy into Classical unemployment. Likewise, a real shock which lowered the Walrasian equilibrium real wage, for instance, the oil price shocks of the 1970s are obvious candidates, would have the same effect when real wages are sticky.)

The third aspect to the policy debate again turns on the difference between the derivations of the aggregate supply functions. Even if the debate is settled one way or another with respect to the use of demand management policies in facilitating the movement of the economy to Y^*, there remains a substantial difference over the merits of Y^*. With the Friedman/Lucas derivation it is the full employment level of output, in the sense that it is what would obtain in the Walrasian equilibrium. From this perspective, the worries over Y^* are of second-order significance. To be sure, as Friedman (1968) himself made plain, the presence of monopoly elements and other sources of distortion from the competitive ideal might provide reasons for government intervention to secure a competitive Walrasian equilibrium. Thus, in so far as there are reasons for disquiet over Y^*, they tend to give rise to the supply-side policies which are designed to secure the operation of competitive markets.

This contrasts with the supply-side economics which flows from NAIRU and the Keynesian derivation of the aggregate supply function. With the wage and price dynamics specified in equations 3.5 to 3.8, it is most unlikely that Y^* will have many desirable properties (see section 3.4). So, there is a much stronger prima-facie case here for some sort of supply-side policy. Further, since these dynamics are often thought to have arisen because of unavoidable features of market economies (see Chapters 6 and 7 and the brief discussion in section 3.4), the policies are not typically directed at achieving some 'mythical' competitive ideal. The competitive ideal cannot be achieved by the government withdrawing from the economy. A full-blown competitive economy actually depends on a range of institutions, like the auctioneer, which even the most interventionist government could not supply. Instead, governments must combat the more obvious sources of market failure through judicious interventions. The list here can very quickly become long, but it needs serious attention, particularly if a rise in NAIRU is to be avoided when there are adverse supply-side shocks. I will just mention two broad classes. Any policy which has an effect on productivity will influence the location of the F function in Figure 3.7. Likewise, policies that affect the bargaining process (either by altering the bargaining power of either party or by changing the institutional context, as for instance through the introduction of an incomes policy) will influence the location of the W curve.

In short, the final strand in the debate over unemployment policy again relates to the microfoundations of the aggregate supply function and concerns the possible role for supply-side policies in securing a desirable level for the non-inflationary output level/'natural' rate.

3.6 Summary of Part 1

One can imagine two sorts of microfoundations for macroeconomics. One has competitive markets with prices moving to clear the markets at the Walrasian equilibrium, except when agents make expectational errors. The other begins from a state of imperfect competition, not necessarily because there are only a few traders in each market, although this may be the case, but because there is imperfect information and agents set prices for a discrete period of time. In such an economy, prices are set by individuals and firms as part of calculations which take into account the likely actions of others and trades will often occur at 'false' prices.

The analysis of the origins of unemployment differs according to the choice of microfoundations. Under the competitive, market clearing choice, output and employment only deviate from full employment when the real wage departs from its Walrasian equilibrium value. Under the other, unemployment can, in addition, be caused by nominal wages and prices deviating from their Walrasian equilibrium values. Yet, somewhat surprisingly in view of these differences, both sets of microfoundations yield what appears to be a formally identical AD/AS macroeconomic model. And from this perspective, one may be inclined to think that the choice of microfoundations will be 'neither here nor there' as far as the debate over unemployment in the AD/AS model is concerned. However, nothing could be further from the truth.

The unemployment debate turns quite critically, in one way or another, on the choice of microfoundations and the related assumptions with respect to expectation formation. To put the issues bluntly: the speed of adjustment of wages, prices and price expectations affects how long the economy is away from the NAIRU/'natural' rate after a demand shock in the AD/AS model and the magnitude of the output deviation during this period of adjustment. I have suggested that greater sluggishness with respect to prices seems likely under the imperfectly competitive rather than the market clearing Walrasian view of wage and price determination. Thus imperfectly competitive microfoundations favour demand management activism. This argument is developed at length in Chapters 6 and 7 where the case for sticky, imperfectly competitive determined prices and wages is advanced. The related competing arguments over expectation formation aspect of this issue are addressed in the next two chapters.

Finally, we have seen that the choice of microfoundations impacts upon the supply-side debate. In particular, the NAIRU which emerges under imperfect competition enjoys none of the normative properties of the 'natural' rate which comes from market clearing competitive microfoundations. Thus, any presumption in favour of imperfectly competitive microfoundations is also likely to count for supply-side activism directed at improving NAIRU.

3.7 Brief Notes on the Literature

The original insight with respect to how labour demand is constrained by aggregate demand is usually credited to Patinkin (1965), while Clower (1965) is credited with making explicit the influence of the constraint in labour markets on final demand – although, to be fair, Keynes (1936) like most of the interpretations of Keynes is the crucial source! Barro and Grossman (1971) connected both constraints, and Malinvaud (1977) provides a well-known generalization and discussion.

The path of adjustment argument in the debate over unemployment policy is famously discussed in Tobin (1975) and has recently been developed further by Hahn and Solow (1989).

Evidence for normal cost pricing is to be found in Coutts, Godley and Nordhaus (1978) and the target real wage and normal cost pricing hypothesis combine, for instance, in Layard and Nickell (1986).

PART 2

The New Classicals and the New Keynesians

4. The New Classical Macroeconomics

4.1 Introduction

Two central NCM arguments against Keynesian activism are set out in this chapter. The first is the famous policy impotence proposition which comes from combining rational expectations with a natural rate model of aggregate supply. It suggests that no systematic aggregate demand management policy, of a Keynesian or any other variety, will have a determinate effect on output.

The second focuses on the adverse effects of discretionary policies on the rate of inflation. Not only does government discretion add to the informational problems faced by the private sector without producing any determinate effect on output, but it can also lead to the adoption of a monetary policy yielding pareto sub-optimal, high rates, of inflation. This argument turns on what is sometimes referred to as a problem of time inconsistency and can be most easily appreciated through a formal analysis of what is, in effect, a game played between the private sector and the government.

The fourth and fifth sections extend the New Classical perspective by presenting a couple of their models of the business cycle. These are important because it is tempting to think that the phenomenon of the business cycle undermines the NCM analysis of policy impotence. After all, if output only deviates from the natural rate when there are expectational errors (the natural rate hypothesis) and rational expectations requires that these errors should not be serially correlated, how are we to generate an account of serially correlated output movements? The NCM models of the business cycle supply an answer and accordingly are important complements to the policy impotence result.

4.2 Policy Impotence/Neutrality

There are two hallmarks of NCM. One is the adoption of the competitive microfoundations which were used in Chapter 2 to derive the Friedman/Lucas (natural rate) version of the aggregate supply function. The assumption that prices move to clear markets is often motivated by the thought that there is something perverse about making the alternative assumption that prices are often set at non-clearing values since non-market clearing prices seem to imply a failure by market participants to realize all potentially mutual beneficial exchanges. As one New Classical pointedly suggested, you do not find £10 notes laying around on the pavement, so why build the equivalent of a world littered with £10 notes into economic models? After all, the reason you do not find £10 notes out on the street is, of course, because people see the opportunity for gain by picking them up. Accordingly, we should assume that agents in markets seize the opportunities available to them and so work with an assumption that prices move to clear markets. At first sight, this looks like a compelling argument. I shall return to it in Chapter 6 because New Keynesians contend that sticky prices are perfectly compatible with rational behaviour in this sense and this leads them to favour imperfectly competitive micro-foundations. For now the argument can be left here as enough has been said to motivate the New Classical position.

The second feature of NCM is the use of the rational expectations hypothesis. I remarked in Chapter 2 that the adaptive expectations hypothesis produces the peculiar result of individuals making systematic errors. The New Classicals build on this observation. Surely, they argue, no rational agent will entertain an expectation which she or he knows will lead to error which could be avoided. Yet this is what is implied when agents use an expectations generating mechanism which produces systematic errors. Surely, to continue the argument, if errors are systematic, then in principle you ought to be able to learn what is driving the systematic component and thereby revise your expectations to remove the systematic element. Furthermore, rational agents will have every incentive to do precisely this since they will thereby profit by holding better expectations. Hence, the argument runs, rational agents will only settle for expectations generating procedures which generate random, white noise errors, since only these sort of errors cannot be anticipated. In short, only these sort of errors are not knowingly entertained when they could be avoided and so the rational expectations hypothesis is captured by

$$P_t^e = P_t + u_t \qquad (4.1)$$

where u_t is a random, white noise error term (that means it has an expected value of zero, $E(u_t)=0$, and there is no serial correlation in the errors so that a positive/negative error in one time period does not make it any more or less likely that there will be a positive/negative error in a subsequent time period, $E(u_i u_j)=0$ for all i and $j \neq 0$).

The policy impotence proposition can now be stated quite simply, if a little loosely. In effect, the rational expectations hypothesis means that the economy is always operating on the vertical aggregate supply function but for random and serially uncorrelated perturbations. Thus, demand management can have no systematic effect on output as the economy only ever randomly deviates from Y^*.

To be slightly more specific, any systematic government management of aggregate demand will produce movements in the AD function which are anticipated. Rational agents will revise their price expectations to take account of the policy effects on prices: and in so doing, they will neutralize the effects of the policy on output and employment. Consider, for instance, some systematic policy in Figure 4.1, a simple Keynesian one, say, which involves increasing aggregate demand by some amount whenever output is below some target value; and suppose this produces a shift in aggregate demand from AD_1 to AD_2.

Figure 4.1   Aggregate demand and aggregate supply

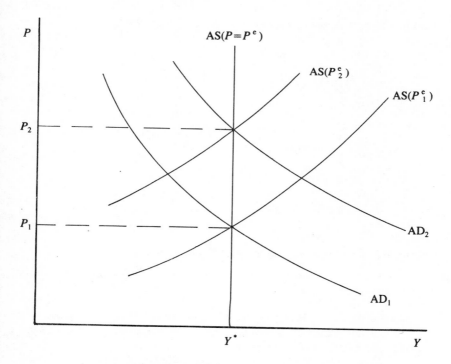

The New Classicals argue that since this shift in AD is the result of a systematic (non-random) policy, it will be anticipated and once it has been anticipated the only rational expectation to hold for prices is P_2^e. Any other price expectation would lead agents knowingly to make an error which they could avoid. Agents need only consult the AD/AS model to see this. If they acted on any other price expectation, this model predicts a price which deviates from that price expectation. The only price expectation which if acted upon in that model yields a prediction for the price which does not deviate from that price expectation is P_2^e. Hence, with these price expectations, the output effects of this aggregate demand shift are completely neutralized. Indeed, the only type of policy change which would have output effects would be one that could not have been predicted by rational agents. But, the only type of change which could not be predicted is a purely random one. So, the only effective policies are the capricious and unsystematic ones which spring surprises on the private sector – but nobody (not even madcap Keynesians) has ever argued for these!

This argument will now be formally developed using the log linear AD/AS model set out in section 2.6. Equations 4.2 to 4.4 are a stochastic version of that model. The AS, IS and LM functions are now subject to independent random white noise disturbance terms in recognition of the vagaries of decision making in the real world which produce random variations in demand and supply decisions from one period to the next.

$$y_t = y^* + a_0(p_t - p_t^e) + u_{it} \tag{4.2}$$

$$y_t = b_0[r_t - (p_{t+1}^e - p_t^e)] + b_1 g_t + u_{2t} \tag{4.3}$$

$$m_t = p_t + c_0 y_t + c_1 r_t + u_{3t} \tag{4.4}$$

Solving 4.2 to 4.4 for the reduced form in p yields

$$p_t = \{p_t^e \ [a_0(c_1 + b_0 c_0) + b_0 c_1] - b_0 c_1 p_{t+1}^e + b_0 m_t + b_1 c_1 g_t$$
$$- (c_0 + b_0 c_0) + c_1 u_{2t} - b_0 u_{3t} - (c_1 + b_0 c_0)u_{1t}\} / [a_0(c_1 + b_0 c_0) + b_0] \tag{4.5}$$

and with a replacement of the composite parameters by d_i, this becomes

$$p_t = d_0 p_t^e + d_1 p_{t+1}^e + d_2 m_t + d_3 g_t + u_{4t} \tag{4.6}$$

where u_{4t} is itself a random white noise error term since it is a weighted sum of three independent white noise error terms. Agents forming rational expectations will wish to avoid entertaining an expectation which knowingly leads to an error. So, they choose an expectation which they predict, using equation 4.6, will only suffer from white noise errors ($p^e = p + u$). This will be achieved through holding the expectation given implicitly by

$$p_t^e = d_0 p_t^e + d_1 p_{t+1}^e + d_2 m_t + d_3 g_t \tag{4.7}$$

To see this result, subtract 4.7 from 4.6 to derive the implied error in expectation. One obtains a random white noise term, u_{4t}.

Let us suppose that monetary and fiscal policy stance are not known with certainty, so that agents must form expectations about m and g before they can form an expectation of p. Thus, 4.7 becomes

$$p_t^e = d_0 p_t^e + d_1 p_{t+1}^e + d_2 m_t^e + d_3 g_t^e \qquad (4.8)$$

and the error in price expectations, through subtraction from 4.6, is

$$p - p_t^e = d_2(m_t - m_t^e) + d_3(g_t - g_t^e) + u_{4t} \qquad (4.9)$$

Suppose further that the government follows a Keynesian-type policy rule so that the money supply increases/decreases whenever output is below/above some target value (y'); and likewise fiscal policy, as in

$$m_t = m_{t-1} + f_0(y' - y_{t-1}) + u_{5t} \qquad (4.10)$$

$$g_t = g_{t-1} + f_1(y' - y_{t-1}) + u_{6t} \qquad (4.11)$$

where u_{5t} and u_{6t} are independent random white noise terms which arise through policy execution errors.

Rational individuals will learn about these policy rules and form their expectations based upon them, thus

$$m_t^e = m_{t-1} + f_0(y' - y_{t-1}) \qquad (4.12)$$

$$g_t^e = g_{t-1} + f_1(y' - y_{t-1}) \qquad (4.13)$$

Consequently, the terms in the brackets of 4.9 will be independent random white noise (u_{5t} and u_{6t}; and the overall error in price expectation is again random white noise because it comprises of the weighted addition of three independent white noise terms. When 4.9 is substituted back into 4.1, I obtain an expression for output movements

$$y_t = y^* + a_0(d_2 u_{5t} + d_3 u_{6t} + u_{4t}) + u_{1t}$$

which shows that output only deviates in a random white noise fashion from the 'natural' rate. Notice, there is no trace in this equation of the systematic policy terms in equations 4.10 and 4.11 (f_0 and f_1). Systematic policy ceases to have an effect because its influence on the price level has been anticipated; and once price changes are anticipated, they fail to cause a movement in output with the natural rate hypothesis. In summary, systematic policy rules of whatever variety are impotent in this world of rational expectations and market clearing price movements.

Of course, some care is required here in drawing this bald conclusion. We have not yet solved 4.7 (or 4.8) for the actual rational expectation for prices. We have been able to derive the impotence result with the implicit solution alone, and this does beg a question about how agents in the real world actually solve this equation. This is a difference equation and its solution is no simple matter when monetary and fiscal policies can change in the future with the election of new governments and when the structural equations of the economy may also evolve. To appreciate this one can approach the solution through a recursive substitution of 4.7/4.8 into itself. The current price level becomes a geometric weighted sum of current and all future expected policy stances. Provided the index of the geometric weight, $d_1/(1-d_0)$, is less than one, these future policy variables will have a dwindling affect on current prices and can eventually be ignored. Nevertheless, it seems that the NCM is making rather Herculean demands here on the average agent in the economy. They must know not only the structural equations of the current economy and the policy rule of the current government, but they must also form expectations for some future set of structural equations and policy rules.

In its defence the NCM might argue that in any complex economy there is a division of labour. And just as we do not expect every individual to provide for his or her own food, clothing, housing, etc., with his or her own hands, so we should not expect every individual to collect the information on the economy and process it to form a rational expectation. There is specialization and there is trade, and we should expect the same with respect to information processing activities: specialist agencies will (and do) develop to serve the needs of the community.

The difficulties with the formation of rational expectations constitute one of the launching pads for the New Keynesian Macroeconomics. Consequently, I shall leave further discussion of this until Chapter 5. I turn now to the other major argument against demand activism which has been mounted by NCM.

4.3 Time Inconsistency with the Optimal Policy

Government discretion with respect to the conduct of macroeconomic policy clearly adds to the informational difficulties which the private sector faces in the formation of a rational expectation. It is one more thing that the private sector has to collect and process information on, and becomes one more source of white noise errors in price expectations which produce white noise deviations of output from its natural level (see equation 4.9). Since these discretionary policies have no systematic effect on output in the NCM and since there is no merit in white noise perturbations, it seems that it would be for the best if the government were to acknowledge the impotence result and forsake discretion in the conduct of its policy.

This line of argument is strengthened by a further NCM consideration. To bring this out, let us assume that the government has an objective function which it attempts to maximize through the choice of its monetary policy when it has discretion over policy. This objective function is given by

$$U_g = -\dot{P}^2 + 2(Y - Y^*)$$
(4.14)

There is nothing special about the precise form of this function and the value of the parameters; it has been chosen because of its algebraic simplicity. But it captures a fairly general idea that governments, for electoral reasons, dislike inflation while they like low unemployment.

I also assume that the natural rate hypothesis governs the relation between inflation and unemployment in the form of

$$\dot{P} = Y - Y^* + \dot{P}^e$$
(4.15)

Finally, I capture the idea that the private sector wishes to form rational expectations with the assumption that it maximizes

$$U_p = -(\dot{P} - \dot{P}^e)^2$$
(4.16)

The government has discretion over monetary policy and thereby sets the rate of inflation in the economy. So we can represent the government's choice as the maximization of 4.14 subject to the constraint in 4.15. This yields a choice for the rate of inflation equal to 1 – since the precise choice of functions here was arbitrary, this can be thought of more generally as a decision to have a positive rate of inflation (that is, non-zero). The pay-off from this decision depends on what rate of inflation the private sector expects and this is determined by the maximization of 4.16. This is maximized by expecting a rate of 1 in these circumstances (that is, the formation of a rational expectation), and so the pay-off to the government is −1.

· Thus I obtain the result that there will be inflation in this economy as a result of maximizing behaviour on the part of the government and the private sector. However, it is plain that there is a superior outcome which was available for this economy. Had the government chosen not to inflate ($\dot{P}=0$), and had the private sector anticipated this: the private sector would enjoy the same pay-off as before but the government would enjoy a superior pay-off of 0. This raises a puzzle. Why did the government choose to inflate as a result of a maximizing calculation when this leads to an inferior outcome? We can answer this question most easily by examining the choice in a game theoretic context. In effect, the government and the private sector are playing a game with each other because the pay-off to each of choosing a rate of inflation and to expecting a rate of inflation, respectively, depends on the actions of the other. Figure 4.2 illustrates this dependence.

Figure 4.2 Macro policy game

government

		$\dot{P}=0$	$\dot{P}=1$
private	$\dot{P}^e=0$	0, 0	-1, 1
sector	$\dot{P}^e=1$	-1, -2	0, -1

In the analysis of a one-shot game, like this, it is often assumed that the players have common knowledge and common rationality. This means that they each know the structure of pay-offs and they each know that the other knows; and that each is instrumentally rational and believes the other also to be rational in this optimizing sense. So, each individual will reason about the game in a manner which duplicates the reasoning of the other and each agent takes this into account when deciding what to do. In these circumstances, game theorists typically argue that a Nash equilibrium, defined as a pair of strategies which are best replies to each other, is the appropriate equilibrium concept – since only when each plays a Nash strategy can each hold consistent conjectures about the other in the manner which is to be expected when there is common knowledge and common rationality.

The Nash equilibrium in this game for $[\dot{P}^e, \dot{P}]$ is $[1, 1]$, but it is pareto-dominated by the $[0, 0]$ strategy pair. The difficulty for the government is that it cannot credibly commit itself to what is the optimal plan of zero inflation because this plan is not time consistent. If the government once persuaded the private sector to expect zero inflation, then the government would want to renege on the commitment because it thereby obtains an even better outcome, a pay-off of 1 rather than 0. The private sector realizes this and does not believe any anti-inflationary statement that the government might use to persuade it to the contrary – after all, they would say that wouldn't they! So the private sector expects inflation. The government, in turn, realizes this and accepts inflation as the best available option.

The optimal outcome would only be available to the economy if the government had its ability to choose an inflationary policy taken away –

perhaps through an independent central bank or joining a fixed exchange rate regime where the dominant country had an independent central bank. In short, the government here must, like Ulysses when he tied himself to the mast, forsake the freedom of discretionary action in order to obtain the best results.

This is an interesting twist on the basic policy impotence result and we shall develop the argument further in the next section as we turn to the NCM models of the business cycle.

4.4 A NCM Political Business Cycle

The policy impotence result suggests that there should only be white noise deviations of output from its 'natural' value, and this appears to pose some difficulty for NCM when we turn to the medium term. After all, one rarely disputed empirical fact is that output movements are serially correlated. Likewise, we actually observe alternating phases of high and low inflation in many countries and yet the time inconsistency results seems to suggest that, in the absence of switches between institutional arrangements which allow discretion and those that do not, we should observe either high or low inflation. In short, there are business cycles and it is not obvious, at first sight, how these features of the cycle can be accommodated by a NCM. Consequently, much theoretical effort in NCM has been concerned with models of the medium term that preserve the basic elements of the analysis, rational expectations and market clearing prices, while generating behaviour which corresponds to that of the business cycle.

In this section, I shall focus on a NCM explanation of the alternating pattern of nominal shocks: that is, the alternating periods of high and low inflation. In the next section, I turn to the explanations of the serial correlation in output movements. I begin with the alternating phases of high and low inflation because the analysis involves a development of the recent discussion of time inconsistency.

It is tempting to think that the problem of credibility in that discussion is altered dramatically once the game is repeated a number of times – and indeed, it seems natural to think of the game being repeated both because governments are often re-elected and because policy is set several times within a term of office. In particular, one might suspect that although it is costly for the government to forego inflation in a single time period, in the sense that the best action is to inflate, it can make sense for the government to forego the best short-run policy if it thereby develops a reputation for non-inflation which enables it to achieve the pareto-superior non-inflationary outcome in subsequent plays of the game. In other words, the long-run interest in the non-inflationary outcome in future plays of the game could outweigh the short-run gain from producing an unanticipated inflation now.

As tempting as this thought may seem, it needs to be handled with care. First, one must distinguish between whether the game is to be repeated a finite or an infinite/indefinite number of times. In the latter case, in any play of the game there is always some positive probability that it will be played again. So there is no definite last play of the game and a forward-looking calculation which compares short-run costs with long-run gains (along the lines that I have just sketched) makes perfect sense. In fact, in such repeated games, there are multiple perfect equilibria and some could produce the non-inflation outcome. (The perfect equilibrium concept requires that strategies should also be in Nash equilibrium for each of the sub-games formed by advancing one stage down the repeated sequence, and it is typically regarded as the appropriate development of the Nash equilibrium concept for these dynamic games.) The multiplicity result is usually referred to as the Folk Theorem and it is not difficult to see why it arises. When a game is repeated infinitely/indefinitely players can develop any number of complicated conditional/punishment strategies, that is strategies which make play in any one period depend on what happened in the previous plays of the game; and so there are many more possible combinations of strategies which can be pursued by players than in the one shot version where each player has a choice between only two strategies.

To illustrate the potential for a perfect equilibrium with non-inflation, consider a rather simple punishment strategy that could be followed by the private sector – it is sometimes referred to as 'trigger'. Here the private sector expects no inflation so long as it does not experience inflation, but if it should experience inflation then thereafter it expects inflation. In these circumstances, in any period, the government will weigh the gain from unanticipated inflation in that period ($= 1$) with the expected present discounted value of the consequent inflationary as opposed to a non-inflationary outcome in all subsequent periods ($= \sum_i d^i(-1)$), where d is an amalgam of the discount rate and the probability of the game being repeated and which are assumed to be constant for all periods). When $d > \frac{1}{2}$, this comparison leads the government not to inflate because the expected present discounted loss in future periods from having inflation rather than non-inflation exceeds the short-run gain from an unanticipated inflation in the current period.

This is an informal demonstration of how one might explain the occurrence of non-inflation. To explain how a non-inflation might give way to inflation, one has to suggest why a government might revise its calculation. The simplest story that might be told turns on the government revising its probability assessment of playing the game again consequent upon the receipt of some new information – perhaps, an opinion poll which is relevant to its likelihood of winning the next election. In turn, this leads d to be revised downwards below $\frac{1}{2}$ and the government decides to inflate. This is not implausible, but there are two important qualifications. The analysis needs to be supplemented by some account of how one perfect equilibrium comes to be selected from amongst the many. I shall have more to say on this in the next chapter and I leave the discussion until then. Furthermore, the assumption of finite repetition looks more attractive than infinite/indefinite one since some electoral systems set explicit limits on re-election and in other cases mortality would seem to make it difficult to hold a belief that in any future play of the game there will always be some probability of the game being repeated. However, once we turn to finitely repeated games, the analysis is significantly different.

When a game is finitely repeated the forward-looking intuition which we have relied on breaks down because there is a last play of the game. In these circumstances, game theorists have used the logic of backward induction to construct the equilibrium for the repeated version of the game. Consider the last play of this game. The government has no need for a reputation of being a non-inflater beyond this play since there is no further play. Thus the last play is exactly like a one shot play of the game; and, consequently, the government will inflate. The private sector realizing this will expect inflation in the last play, and so the government has no need to worry about carrying a reputation for non-inflation from the penultimate play of the game through to the last. This makes the penultimate play of the game also like a one shot play, where there is no regard for reputation, and the government will inflate in this play as well. The private sector realizes this and so expects inflation, and this means the government has no need to worry about carrying a reputation for non-inflation through from the previous play – and so on. The game unzips back from the last play to the first play with inflation which is expected at all times.

This is genuinely puzzling because we often have a strong intuition that things are different when we repeat them, even if only finitely. And there is an equally strong feeling that we do observe reputation creating behaviour in the real world. Fortunately, our intuitions can be rescued by allowing for some doubt over the motives of the government; and this has interesting consequences for the understanding of the business cycle.

Let us assume that there is some probability, q, that the government has a different objective function, one which values non-inflation above all else. The pay-offs for such a government are captured in Figure 4.3.

Figure 4.3 Macro policy game with a 'hard-nosed' government

government

		$\dot{P}=0$	$\dot{P}=1$
private sector	$\dot{P}^e=0$	0, 0	−1, −1
	$\dot{P}^e=1$	−1, 0	0, −1

The key to an alternative analysis of the game now comes through recognizing that should $q \geq \frac{1}{2}$ in the last play of the game, then it is no longer certain that private sector will expect inflation in that play of the game. To appreciate this, consider the respective expected returns from expecting zero inflation and expecting inflation in the last play: these returns are identical when $q = \frac{1}{2}$. Hence it ceases to be certain when $q = \frac{1}{2}$ that the private sector will expect inflation in the last play and the moment this is no longer certain the backward induction process cannot take hold to produce the inflation/expected inflation result for all periods. Instead, there are alternative equilibria. In particular, if we assume that the private sector uses a Bayesian updating rule for beliefs, then it turns out that what is referred to as a sequential equilibrium can arise in this game with characteristics of a business cycle even when initially q is considerably less than $\frac{1}{2}$. In this sequential equilibrium, there can be an initial period of non-inflation, which can then be followed by unanticipated inflation, and which concludes with an anticipated inflation. In short, we might observe alternating phases of non-inflation and inflation during the life of a single government. I shall offer a sketch of the proof of this proposition here.

First, let me introduce some notation. The last play of the game occurs in time period T; and so, in time period t, there are $T-t+1$ plays remaining in the game. To avoid confusions between the probability operator P and the rate of inflation, let x_t stand for the rate of inflation. Let y_t be the probability that a 'wet' (W) government (that is a government with pay-offs like those in Figure 4.2 as contrasted with the 'hard-nosed' variety (HN) in Figure 4.3) does not inflate; and let z_t be the probability that the private sector expects non-inflation in t. Finally, there is Bayes's Rule which comes in two parts in this instance:

1. When there has been inflation (i.e. $x_t = 1$), then $q_{t+1} = 0$.
2. When there has not been inflation (i.e. $x_t = 0$), then

$$q_{t+1} = P(\text{HN} | x_t = 0)$$

$$= P(\text{HN and } x_t = 0)/P(x_t = 0)$$

$$= P(x_t = 0 | \text{HN}).P(\text{HN})/[P(x_t = 0 | \text{HN}).P(\text{HN}) + P(x_t = 0 | W).p(W)]$$

$$= 1.q_t/[q_t + (1 - q_t)y_t] \tag{4.17}$$

One comment is worth making about Bayes's Rule because it imparts an important character to the sequential equilibrium result: q only ever increases when $y_t < 1$. This means that reputation creating behaviour (specifically the choice of y_t here to influence q_{t+1}) is risky for a 'wet' government since it must adopt a strategy of inflating with some positive probability to improve its reputation for being 'hard-nosed'. This may seem somewhat strange at first, but on reflection it does make sense. If a 'wet' government always did not inflate, then the observation of non-inflation would provide no reason for updating your belief about the nature of the government since 'hard-nosed' never inflate as well. For the observation of non-inflation to provide a reason for updating your beliefs about the government then this outcome must be one that is more likely for 'hard-nosed' than a 'wet' government and this will only be the case when there is some positive probability that a 'wet' government will inflate. A corollary of this risk is that the government will not wish to build a reputation until it becomes absolutely necessary.

For notational simplicity let $s_t = q_t + (1-q_t) y_t$, thus Bayes's Rule under 2. above becomes

$$q_{t+1} = q_t/s_t \tag{4.18}$$

Now, consider the expected return to the private sector in some period t when there is still doubt over the government's identity (that is q_t is not zero). It is given by

$$\begin{aligned}
E(U_{pt}) = {} & z_t\{q_t(0)+(1-q_t)[y_t(0)+(1-y_t)(-1)]\} \\
& +(1-z_t)\{q_t(-1)+(1-q_t)[y_t(-1)+(1-y_t)(0)]\} \\
& +[q_t+(1-q_t)y_t]E(U_{pt+1})
\end{aligned} \tag{4.19}$$

This can be checked by decomposing the return into the expected return from this play of the game (= return when the private sector expects inflation × the probability of expecting inflation + the return when the private sector does not expect inflation × the probability of not expecting inflation) + the expected return from future plays of the game (=expected return from future plays when there is still doubt in the private sector's mind × the probability that there will remain doubt after this play of the game + the expected return when there is no doubt, which is 0). With some rearrangement and the substitution for s_t, this becomes

$$E(U_{pt}) = z_t(2s_t-1)-s_t+s_tE(U_{pt+1}) \tag{4.20}$$

Through inspection of 4.20, it is clear that this expression is maximized through a choice of $z_t=1$ when $s_t>\frac{1}{2}$, and $z_t=0$ when $s_t<\frac{1}{2}$, and there is indifference over the choice of z_t when $s_t=\frac{1}{2}$.

This observation together with 4.18 enables us to construct a locus of the values for q, one for each time period which will: (a) leave the private sector indifferent between expecting and not expecting inflation; and (b) remain consistent with $q_T = \frac{1}{2}$. Consider q_{T-1}, it follows from 4.18 that $q_T = \frac{1}{2}$ can be obtained with the government choosing y_{T-1} to achieve $s_{T-1} = \frac{1}{2}$ (for private sector indifference) when $q_{T-1} = (\frac{1}{2})^2$. (Notice, should q exceed this value, then it follows from 4.18 that the government can set s at a higher value than $\frac{1}{2}$ and still achieve the terminal value of $\frac{1}{2}$ to prevent backward induction taking hold; and from 4.20 it follows that the private sector will expect zero inflation in these circumstances.) Now consider time $T-2$, the value of q_{T-2} which is consistent with achieving the value of $q_T = \frac{1}{2}$ and which just leaves the private sector indifferent between expecting and not expecting inflation can be calculated using the earlier result for q_{T-1}: $s_{T-2} = \frac{1}{2}$ for indifference and $q_{T-1} = (\frac{1}{2})^2$ to maintain the path for q where the private sector is indifferent; and thus from 4.18 we obtain $q_{T-2} = (\frac{1}{2})^3$. (Notice again, when q exceeds this value in $T-2$, the government can set s in $T-2$ at a value greater than $\frac{1}{2}$ and still remain consistent with the possibility of achieving a terminal q of $\frac{1}{2}$, and so in this circumstance the private sector will expect zero inflation.) Figure 4.4 plots the locus of values for q obtained by repeating this argument

Figure 4.4 Reputation building in sequential equilibrium

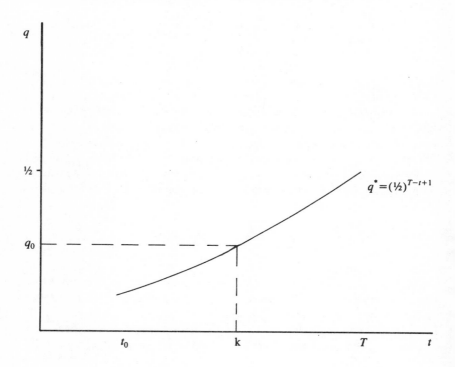

in each time period. I define the crucial q in each time period as q^* and it is given by the function $q_t^* = \frac{1}{2}^{T-t+1}$.

With this function in place, we can see how a sequential equilibrium in the game is constructed. Let us suppose the initial doubt in t_0 about the motives of the government is captured by q_0. This exceeds the crucial value of q^* in that period and so the private sector knows there is insufficient probability of the government inflating to warrant the expectation of inflation. In fact, the government will not have to risk inflation until time k because only at this point does the value of q have to begin to rise to remain consistent with the potential achievement of a terminal value of $\frac{1}{2}$. Since it is risky to build a reputation by setting $y_t < 1$, the government will not attempt to build its reputation until it is absolutely necessary (that is, in time k). Thus until k, there is no inflation and no expected inflation.

Once k has been reached, the government has to start building a reputation by setting $y < 1$ and the private sector will also begin to randomize between expecting and not expecting inflation. If the government does not inflate, the value of q rises along the path described by q^* and the same thing happens in the next time period. It should be noted that this increase in the value of q may or may not be accompanied by a recession because the private sector is randomizing between expecting and not expecting inflation and so it is possible that it expected inflation when none occurred with the result that output dips below the natural rate (or the NAIRU value). Alternatively, if the government inflates once reputation building has begun, then its reputation is dashed and thereafter there will be inflation which is expected in all remaining plays of the game. It should be noted that when this loss reputation occurs it can be accompanied by an expansion of output because the private sector is randomizing and may not expect the inflation when it occurs.

To summarize, there is a period of non-inflation which is expected during the early part of the term of office. How long this lasts depends on the degree of doubt about motives entertained by the private sector. Thereafter, there is a period of reputation building and this can be accompanied by a recession or it can terminate abruptly after an inflation, that may have produced an expansion in output because the inflation was not expected. Once a reputation has been dashed by an inflation, the remainder of the game is characterized by inflation which is expected.

From this summary, it will be clear how it contains the kernel of an explanation of a political business cycle in the sense that there is the potential for the rhythmic alternation of macroeconomic policy which we associate with the cycle. There is an early period of non-inflation and it becomes increasingly likely that this will give way to a period of inflation as the game proceeds, and during this period of potential transition there may be recessions followed by expansions of output.

4.5 Models of the Real Business Cycle

Inflation mistakes may occur in the model of the last section and when they do, there will be output movements. However, there is no explanation there of why such output movements should be serially correlated. Once a mistake has been made by the private sector in one period there is no reason to believe it becomes more likely that the private sector will make the same mistake again. There is no persistence as such. I turn to this aspect of the business cycle in this section.

The general strategy of the NCM is to posit a variety of reasons why a shock which affects output in one period might persist for a number of subsequent periods. Although many of the mechanisms considered by NCM apply equally well to nominal shocks, like the monetary changes of the last section, the NCM has tended to focus on real shocks, changes in tastes, surges in productivity, and so on. The business cycles which emerge are 'real' business cycles because they are caused by real shocks and it is the movements in the 'natural' rate which explain the appearance of business cycles in the data on output.

There are many models in this tradition. For instance, one line of argument turns on how a random surge in productivity raises output in the period in which it occurs and this leads to higher savings and capital accumulation than would otherwise have been the case. In this way the one-off surge has continuing effects on output in the later periods because there is more capital in place.

Another line of argument turns on the production smoothing effects of firms using inventories to accommodate a shock. Suppose there is a shock which affects tastes and through tastes the demand for commodities in one period. When there are costs of adjustment associated with changing output levels, a firm prefers to cushion such a change by partially responding through a run-down of inventories. Accordingly, output changes in the period of the demand shock, but only by a fraction of the change in demand. In the next time period, the shock to demand is no longer present, but the firm must restore its depleted inventories and so output remains above/below its usual level. In short, the effects of the shock persist in the time series on output.

To illustrate this type of argument I shall consider a version of the representative agent model, which is standardly used in this literature. In these models, all individuals are assumed to be identical and so no trade occurs between individuals and thus the behaviour of the economy in the aggregate is simply the sum of identically behaved 'Robinson Crusoe' like individuals – hence the term representative agent.

1. There are a large number of infinitely lived individuals with identical, log linear and separable utility functions given by

$$U = \sum_{t=0}^{\infty} d^{t}[a\log C_{t}+(1-a)\log(24-L_{t})] \qquad (4.21)$$

where d is a discount factor, C_t and L_t are consumption and labour supplied in time t and a is a parameter.

2.   There is a single commodity that can be produced by the individual using the commodity as capital and labour according to the production function,

$$Y_t = Z_t L_t^b K_t^{1-b} \qquad (4.22)$$

where Z is an index of productivity in this Cobb-Douglas production function and it is a random variable through which we shall incorporate productivity shocks, L_t and K_t are labour supplied and the capital stock in time t, and b is a parameter.

3.   The commodity is perishable after one period and since there will be no trade between individuals, the individual faces a budget constraint in each period of the form

$$C_t + K_{t+1} = Z_t L_t^b K_t^{1-b} \qquad (4.23)$$

4.   The individual chooses a pair (C,L) for each time period so as to maximize the expected value of 4.21 subject to the sequence of constraints implied by 4.23.

The first order conditions for maximization here entail

$$a/C_t = \lambda_t \qquad (4.24)$$

$$(1-a)/(24-L_t) = b\lambda_t Z_t L_t^{b-1} K_t^{1-b} \qquad (4.25)$$

$$\lambda_t = (1-b)Z_{t+1} L_{t+1}^b K_{t+1}^{-b} dE_t \lambda_{t+1} \qquad (4.26)$$

where E_t is the expectation operator conditional on information at t.

$$C_t + K_{t+1} = Z_t L_t^b K_t^{1-b}$$

The first two conditions are the standard ones from one period maximization problems where λ is the marginal utility in that period of an increment in the commodity. Equation 4.26 captures the intertemporal nature of the maximization problem and entails that the marginal disutility of giving up an increment of the commodity in t must be equal to the marginal gain in utility in $t+1$ when discounted back to t which arises from using the fraction of the commodity as additional capital in $t+1$ in the production of the commodity in $t+1$. The last condition is simply the budget constraint again. We also wish to impose a transversality condition,

$$\lim_{j \to \infty} E_t d^{j-1} \lambda_{t+j} K_{t+j+1} = 0 \qquad (4.27)$$

The intuition behind this condition comes from considering the last period in a finite maximization problem. It would plainly not make sense to hold capital over from the last period T since utility can only be enhanced by consuming it in the last period. Equation 4.27 can be thought of as the limit of this same condition as T tends to infinity.

It is not always easy to calculate the solutions to a system of equations like those in 4.23 to 4.27. However, the choice of these particular utility and production functions does produce an analytic solution with some ease. First, notice that with this utility function and the perishability of the commodity after one period, the income and substitution effects of a wage rate change exactly offset each other. Thus, it is plausible to try a solution which has L_t equal to a constant (L'). If this is the case then the form of the production function together with the budget constraint suggest that the solution for C and K might take the following form

$$C_t = eZ_t K_t^{1-b} \qquad (4.28)$$

$$K_{t+1} = fZ_t K_t^{1-b} \qquad (4.29)$$

where e and f are parameters yet to be determined.

This is a conjecture, but we can try to solve for e and f using 4.23 to 4.26 to see whether our conjectures hold up. Indeed this is easy to do and our conjectures prove correct. In particular,

$$C_t = [1-(1-b)d] L^b Z_t K_t^{1-b} \qquad (4.30)$$

$$K_{t+1} = (1-b)dL^b Z_t K_t^{1-b} \qquad (4.31)$$

$$L' = ab/\{ab+(1-a)[1-d(1-b)]\} \qquad (4.32)$$

The interesting feature of this solution to the dynamic utility maximization problem is that 4.31 implies that when the log of $Z_t(z_t)$ is serially uncorrelated (that is, there are random productivity changes), the capital stock will exhibit serial correlation. To appreciate this, we revert to logs and observe that 4.31 defines a stochastic process of the form

$$k_{t+1} = g + (1-b)k_t + z_t$$

and consequently k will exhibit positive serial correlation and with k behaving in this way, it follows that y will also exhibit this pattern. Finally, for the sake of completeness, it may be noted that when z follows a first order autoregressive path, the path for y and k becomes second order autoregressive.

This is a simple but powerful illustration of how white noise real shocks can produce serially correlated output movements. Nevertheless, there are some remaining problems for NCM accounts of the cycle. As it stands, this model does not yield any change in employment over the cycle. The choice of utility function is responsible for this. As productivity surges, so should real wage offers and this might be expected to produce an increase in labour supplied and employment; and vice versa when productivity drops. However, with this particular utility function the income and substitution effects of wage changes exactly cancel and so prevent any employment change. The resolution of the problem seems obvious: we should introduce a more general utility function where the real wage affects labour supply.

However, this is not as straightforward as it might seem. If real wage changes are the mechanism through which we observe cyclical employment variations, why has the secular rise in the real wage not been associated with a rise in the amount of labour supplied (by each individual)? Parenthetically it is worth noting that the 'trading at false prices' school with 'Keynesian' unemployment has no such difficulty reconciling the cyclical with the secular movements of the supply of labour because the level of employment is demand determined over the cycle. The labour supply can be invariant to the real wage and there will still be cyclical movements in the employment when demand moves cyclically and there is trading at false prices.

The way around this problem for NCM is to allow for temporary surges in the real wage to produce a reallocation of leisure across time periods. The supply of labour may not respond to a permanent increase in the real wage, but a temporary boost to the real wage is likely to produce a substitution of work for leisure now, which will be compensated for when real wages drop in the other direction by the individual taking more leisure than usual. Thus, with inventories or capital accumulation and the like linking output movements between periods and the intertemporal reallocation of leisure in response to temporary changes in the real wage, the NCM offers a way of understanding the occurrence of cycles in output and employment.

4.6 Conclusion

This chapter has sketched the main elements of the NCM position. It combines the market clearing prices (competitive microfoundations) with rational expectations to produce two arguments against policy activism of the Keynesian or any other variety. The first is that any activist policy rule, once it is widely known, becomes impotent as far as affecting output is concerned. The second is that not only does activism add to the difficulties faced by the private sector in forming its expectations, but it is also quite likely to yield a sub-optimal outcome for inflation.

These are impressive results and they would seem to count against activism. Yet, at first sight, there are also likely to be doubts because it is not immediately obvious how such a model of the economy can explain the occurrence of business cycles over the medium run. Consequently, much NCM effort has gone into the development of complementary models of the cycle. One strand in this literature is an outgrowth from the time inconsistency problem which is responsible for the sub-optimal inflation result. It offers a potential explanation of a pattern of nominal shocks which might produce the alternating phases of the cycle. As such it belongs to both the tradition of modelling the cycle as a political phenomenon and to a tradition in business-cycle analysis which is most concerned with explaining the alternating phases of the cycle. This contrasts with the Frisch (1933) tradition which focuses on how random white noise shocks can generate serially correlated output movements. It is here that most of the NCM efforts have been channelled. In particular, they focus on how real shocks can be propagated to produce cycle-like movements; and I have presented a detailed illustration of this type of modelling in the last section of the chapter.

4.7 Brief Notes on the Literature

Muth (1961) is credited with introducing rational expectations and Sargent and Wallace (1975) famously produced the policy impotence result. Kydland and Prescott (1977) first posed the problem of time inconsistency with respect to macroeconomic policy. Bacharach (1976) provides an introduction to game theory, Rasmusen (1989) is a more advanced text, and the claims of the Nash equilibrium concept are discussed at greater length in Binmore and Dasgupta (1986). The game theoretic approach to macropolicy has subsequently spawned a large literature. Barro and Gordon (1983) offer one of the first models of a reputational equilibria for an infinitely repeated game and they suggest the possibility of a sequential equilibrium approach for a finitely repeated game. This was formally developed by Backus and Driffill (1985). The sequential equilibrium concept was itself developed by Kreps and Wilson (1982a, 1982b). Robert Lucas is the key figure in the development of the NCM models of the business cycle. Lucas and Rapping (1969) first presented a model with the intertemporal substitution of leisure, and Lucas (1981) contains a number of his most important papers. McCallum (1989) is the source of the discussion of the representative agent model in the last section, and this contains references to most of the landmark papers, like that of Kydland and Prescott (1982).

5. The New Keynesian Macroeconomics I: The Difficulties with Rational Expectations

5.1 Introduction

This chapter focuses on two difficulties with the NCM use of the rational expectations hypothesis. Both difficulties contribute to a revival of the arguments for policy activism – even in economies with competitive microfoundations where prices move freely to equilibrate markets. In fact, to maintain a sharp distinction between these expectational difficulties and the discussion of wage and price stickiness in Chapters 6 and 7, I shall only consider models with competitive microfoundations here.

The first problem concerns the acquisition of a rational expectation when there is learning to be done and it arises because our ignorance affects the very material that we are trying to learn from. The evidence that we use to update our beliefs on the rational expectations relationship between variables comes from the recent behaviour of the economy, but this evidence is itself distorted by our ignorance because our ('faulty') beliefs affect our behaviours and these behaviours contribute in turn to the economic outcomes (that is, the 'evidence' we use to update beliefs). This impregnation of the data used for learning by our own ignorance raises a question of whether we shall ever escape from that ignorance: will the learning process converge? Or will our own ignorance lead us ever further astray? This difficulty is discussed in the next section in the context of a simple model of financial markets.

The connection between the argument for Keynesian activism and this difficulty can be expressed loosely and simply. Should learning fail to converge, the rational expectations hypothesis ceases to be the relevant expectations assumption. The actual formation of expectations then depends on the learning process and since this involves updating on the basis of new evidence, it will for much of the time approximate something like an adaptive expectations hypothesis. And we know from the discussion in Chapters 2 and 3 that models with adaptive expectations offer opportunities for demand management which disappear in the NCM models with rational expectations.

The second problem relates to the selection of a rational expectations equilibrium when there are multiple rational expectations equilibrium. This issue is first addressed in the third section with a model of speculative bubbles in financial markets.

The problem of equilibrium selection encourages a similar policy conclusion. It is tempting to surmise that individuals will be forced back on simple shared rules of thumb, like the adaptive scheme, to fix expectations when there are multiple rational expectations equilibria; and this opens the route to the same argument for Keynesian activism. This is not implausible and it is an important line of argument. Nevertheless, there is more to the NKM on multiple equilibria than this, as we see in sections 5.4 and 5.5.

Section 5.4 presents an overlapping generations model with multiple bootstraps equilibria. In this model, it is possible to make precise sense of both how a change in government policy and/or a change in 'animal spirits' can alter output and employment even when prices move to equilibrate markets and agents hold rational expectations.

These results run directly counter to the NCM model of Chapter 4 and, interestingly, they arise because individuals can hold a variety of self-fulfilling beliefs with respect to the consequences of government policy. In such circumstances, the choice of which self-fulfilling belief to hold must depend on individuals coordinating their beliefs. By definition, the source of the coordination must be extraneous to the economic model since the model itself throws up multiple equilibria; and demand management affects output under some sources of extraneous belief coordination. The general insight here over the role of extraneous belief opens a new dimension to the policy debate. If governments can influence these extraneous sources of belief, then they will be able to affect the behaviour of the economy. Indeed, if a government can act upon this independent level of belief formation, it may have discovered a more potent weapon than the manipulation of aggregate demand. (In suggesting this, there is, of course, more than an echo of the much older idea in the Post Keynesian tradition that 'Keynesianism' may have had its most significant impact on the behaviour of the economy through its influence on the way that the private sector formed expectations rather than through the direct effects of demand management. Consequently, this section might also be thought to provide a rigorous foundation for this proposition.)

Section 5.5 examines some of the more general properties of the overlapping generations model. In particular, it shows how the model can generate cyclical, chaotic and sunspot driven behaviour. This not only affords an alternative explanation of the business cycle to the NCMs in Chapter 4, it also helps to generalize the insights with respect to the potential role of policy directed at influencing extraneous belief formation.

5.2 Acquiring a Rational Expectation

It will be recalled from section 4.2 that the rational expectations hypothesis seemed at first sight to make extraordinary informational demands on individuals. One possible defence of the hypothesis against this charge was presented in that section: it revolved around the likelihood of a division of labour emerging in the acquisition and processing of information. Another possible defence turns on how prices in markets are influenced by private information with the result that the price system itself becomes an aggregator and transmitter of information to people who have not made the investment in the private acquisition of information. This argument is trading on one of the traditional Austrian defences of the market as an efficient transmitter of information. It is interesting in its own right and takes on a new significance in this discussion of rational expectations. I shall examine the idea here with a model of financial markets which can be easily extended to analyse the possible dynamics of expectation formation when there is learning.

I shall assume the following:

1. Individual i has a utility function in wealth held at the end of the decision period given by

$$U(W_i) = -\exp(-k_i W_i) \qquad (5.1)$$

all individuals have similar utility functions in wealth, they only differ according to the parameter k, which is the coefficient of absolute risk aversion, and the original holdings of wealth, W_{i0}.

2. There are two assets in which the individual can hold wealth. One is riskless and yields interest payments at a rate r. The other is a risky asset that can be purchased at a price P. The gross yield on the risky asset (R) is not known and the individual must form expectations of its value, $E(R)$. Let X_i be the number of units of the risky asset purchased by individual i.

3. The return on the risky asset is determined by a process which can be captured by

$$R = I + e \qquad (5.2)$$

where e is a random white noise with expected value of zero.

Thus, those individuals who condition their expectation of R on I will be able to form a rational expectation of R (that is, $E(R|I) = RE(R)$, I shall use this notation (RE) for a rational expectation here as we will be considering a variety of expectations).

4. Each individual decides to distribute initial wealth between the two assets so as to maximize the expected value of utility in 5.1. It follows from 1 and 2 that the final wealth holding is given by

$$W_i = [R-P(1+r)]X_i + W_{i0}(1+r) \qquad (5.3)$$

When wealth is normally distributed the expected utility from 5.1 becomes

$$E[U(W_i)] = -\exp\{-k_i[E(W_i)-1/2k_i\mathrm{var}(W_i)]\} \qquad (5.4)$$

Through inspection, this expression will be maximized when the term in square brackets is maximized. Once it is noted that the var (W) depends on the var (R) and the number of units of the risky asset purchased, X, it follows that the first order conditions for maximization yield the demand for the risky asset

$$X_i = [1/k_i\mathrm{var}(R)][E(R)-P(1+r)] \qquad (5.5)$$

Summing over all individuals, I can obtain the market demand which is equated with supply of the risky asset (S) to yield the following implicit relation in market equilibrium between the price of the asset (P) and its expected return $(E(R))$,

$$\sum_i [1/k_i \mathrm{var}(R)][E(R)-P(1+r)] = S \qquad (5.6)$$

The rational expectations equilibrium relationship between price and expected return is given by substituting $E(R|I)$ into 5.6. This produces

$$E(R|I) = S\mathrm{var}(R)/\Sigma[1/k_i] + (1+r)P \qquad (5.7)$$

or, in effect,

$$RE(R) = a^* + b^*P \qquad (5.8)$$

In short, in the rational expectations equilibrium, an individual who does not have access to the information in I, or who has not made the investment in I, can nevertheless form a rational expectation of R by conditioning that expectation on the publicly-available information, its price, P. The individual who is not informed, only needs to learn the values of the appropriate parameters, a and b, and use 5.8. This is both an extraordinary and perplexing result. It means that there is perfect transmission of private information in the rational expectations equilibrium to uninformed individuals via prices. Prices are extraordinary aggregators and purveyors of information! Yet, there is a puzzle: if you can do as well without information as with it, then why bother to collect it? But, if no one acquires the information, why should the rational expectations equilibrium obtain?

These puzzles can be answered, but they do force a qualification to the perfect transmission result. There must be an incentive for some to acquire the information if there is to be a rational expectations equilibrium and thus the opportunity for the transmission of information from the informed to the uninformed. So, the rational expectation of the informed must be more accurate than the expectation which is conditioned on prices alone. Hence, transmission must be imperfect to some degree. (Indeed, it is not difficult to amend this model to allow for this possibility by turning S, the supply of the risky asset, into a random variable. The uninformed will now condition their expectation on the expected value of S and this will produce errors whenever S deviates from its expected value which will not be made by those who condition their expectation on I.)

Let us now consider the learning process of the uninformed agents in this market. In general, it is not possible to specify a uniquely rational learning process (for reasons which are discussed more fully in Frydman and Phelps, 1983). So, I shall have to specify a particular learning rule. This is somewhat unsatisfactory from the point of view of producing general results. Nevertheless, I suspect the rule that I have chosen will seem reasonably plausible; and it gives the flavour of results which have been generated by a variety of learning processes.

Suppose the uninformed begin with parameter estimates a_0 and b_0, and that they use the implied expectations from 5.8 for a sufficiently long period to generate new observations on R and P which enable statistically meaningful re-estimations of a $(=a_1)$ and b $(=b_1)$. These new parameter estimates are now used for another sufficiently long period until a and b can be re-estimated, and so on. For simplicity, further assume that $r=0$; that the informed have identical utility functions such that $1/k_i$ var $(R) = O_i$; likewise the uninformed such that $1/k_u$ var $(R) = O_u$; and that the numbers of informed and uninformed are respectively N_i and N_u.

With these simplifications, the market equilibrium for any time period t given by 5.6 becomes

$$[E(R|I)-P_t]N_i O_i + (a_0 + b_0 P_t - P_t)N_u O_u = S_t \qquad (5.9)$$

Since, $E(R|I)=R + e$, then 5.9 will yield the following deterministic relationship between R and P

$$R = [(S_t-N_u O_u a_0)/N_i O_i] + P_t[(N_i O_i+N_u O_u-b_0 N_u O_u)/(N_i O_i)] \quad (5.10)$$

This is the relationship which the uninformed individuals will estimate, and provided there are a sufficient number of observations of this relationship, the new parameter estimate for a $(=a_1)$ will be given by the first square brackets and the new parameter estimate for b $(=b_1)$ will be given by the second square brackets. Accordingly, the learning process is captured by difference equations for a and b. These can be usefully simplified by noting from 5.7 and 5.8 the rational expectations values of a (that is, a^*) and b (b^*),

$$a_1 = a^* + (N_u O_u / N_i O_i)(a^* - a_0) \qquad (5.11)$$

$$b_1 = b^* + (N_u O_u / N_i O_i)(b^* - b_0) \qquad (5.12)$$

Hence, a and b will converge on their rational expectation equilibrium values when $N_u O_u / N_i O_i < 1$. That is, when, so to speak, the weight of informed opinion in the market is greater than that of the uniformed. Naturally, the precise conditions for convergence in learning will depend on the precise learning procedure which has been assumed. But, this is a reasonable, ordinary least squares learning process and it produces an intuitively plausible result. After all, the behaviour of the uninformed in the market will affect the observed relationship between P and R and it is possible that their behaviour can so alter this relationship that they become incapable of learning the true rational expectations equilibrium one. Whether they do or not depends on whether the weight of informed opinion dominates, in the sense above, that of the uniformed in determining market outcomes.

Thus, to summarize, a simple model has been used to demonstrate that prices can transmit information, but the transmission will never be perfect when it is costly to acquire information because there must be an incentive in equilibrium for some individuals to acquire information before it can be transmitted. Further, it was shown that learning how to extract information from prices is not necessarily straightforward. In particular, convergence cannot be guaranteed even when there is a unique rational expectation because the behaviour of the uninformed distorts the observed relationship between variables away from that which holds in the rational expectations equilibrium. The importance of this last result for the policy debate is simply that it becomes more realistic to model expectation formation by a learning mechanism than by the rational expectation hypothesis when there is not convergence; and many learning procedures look similar to the adaptive expectations scheme.

5.3 Speculative Bubbles and Sunspots Equilibria

In the last section, I assumed by construction that there was a unique rational expectations equilibrium. This served the purpose there well, but in this section

I want to turn to the difficulties posed by the existence of multiple rational expectations equilibria. Towards this end, let us go back to 5.6. This shows us the market relationship between the expected return and the price of an asset. However, this time I will not assume that the rational expectation for R is given independently by a relationship like the one in 5.2. Instead, I assume that the return comes in the form of a dividend, D, and a possible capital gain/loss arising from a difference between the current and future price of the asset. Equation 5.6 can now be rewritten as,

$$P_t = fC + fD_t + fP^e_{t+1} \qquad (5.13)$$

where $f = 1/(1+r)$, and C is negative. C is, in effect, the risk premium which is paid on the risky asset. It arises in this context because individuals, under the assumption of 5.1, are not risk neutral and must be compensated for holding the risky asset. Indeed, to check on the intuition here, notice that when individuals are risk neutral and $C=0$, 5.13 simply says that the price of the asset must be equal to the present discounted value of its dividend and resale price.

I assume that the conditions affecting C remain constant over time, as does the dividend. In these circumstances, there is a unique stable rational expectations equilibrium. To understand this it should be noted that under rational expectations the expected price must be equal to the actual price but for a white noise error. Accordingly, 5.13 defines a difference equation for prices under rational expectations and the solutions to this equation give both the path for prices and expectations. With C and D constant, it is easy to solve for the stationary value of P in this equation: it is

$$P = (C + D)f/(1-f) \qquad (5.14)$$

However there are also explosive solutions for 5.13. This is easy to appreciate from the structure of 5.13. P_t can be higher than the value in 5.14 provided the expected price in $t+1$ exceeds P_t by a suitable amount (since $f<1$). Such a P^e_{t+1} will be rational if it equals P_{t+1} and P_{t+1} can take on this higher value if P^e_{t+2} is expected to be even higher by a suitable amount, and so on. All that is required is for the time path of prices to show the necessary acceleration and an alternative rational expectations equilibrium is possible. Indeed, there will be one for each possible initial jump of prices above the stationary value in 5.14. These explosive rational expectations equilibria are sometimes referred to as speculative bubbles because it is the expectation of future price rises which bids up current prices, and future price rises are only rationally expected because prices are expected to rise even higher later, and so on. It is the expectation of ever-rising prices that produces prices which spiral.

There is a standard argument against including these unstable rational expectations equilibria. It holds that since prices cannot actually rise for ever without a breakdown of the economy, these paths should be discounted. This argument has some merit, but it is less compelling on reflection. First, the fact that the economy may break down sometime in the future need not deter any individual now from holding an expectation that prices will rise. It is true, of course, that when the breakdown occurs some individuals will find that their previous expectations have been confounded. But this need not be any individual who is currently participating in the economy and whose expectations are responsible for the current acceleration in prices. Indeed, if the breakdown necessarily involves current individuals getting things wrong, then there would be good reasons for discounting these paths. But this is not the case because we do not live forever and, consequently, it is always possible that a future generation will be left to deal with the breakdown.

Second, the argument against spiralling prices has some force because we do not actually observe prices ever accelerating off to infinity. Nevertheless, we often see small speculative bubbles which burst: that is, short accelerations followed by a quick 'correction'; and they are consistent with rational expectations. To appreciate this, consider the general solution to 5.13 given by

$$P_t = (C+D)f/(1-f) + g_t \qquad (5.15)$$

where

$$E(g_{t+1}) = (1/f)\, g_t \qquad (5.16)$$

The unique stable solution occurs when $g_t = 0$ and the explosive solution takes the form $g_t = g_0\,(1/f)^t$, with one explosive path for each possible value of g_0. In addition, there is a probabilistic solution which satisfies the condition 5.16. It is

$$g_t \begin{cases} = (\pi f)^{-1} g_{t-1} + \mu_t, \text{ with probability } \pi \\[2mm] = \mu_t, \text{ with probability } 1-\pi \end{cases} \qquad (5.17)$$

where μ_t is white noise.

Under 5.17, there is a rational expectation bubble which has an expected duration of $(1-\pi)^{-1}$ before it bursts; and there are a potential multiplicity of such bubbles, one for each value of π. These probabilistic solutions are sometimes referred to as 'sunspots' equilibria. The idea behind this description is that individuals might condition their expectation of prices rising on some extraneous event, like sunspot activity. When individuals form expectations in this manner, each individual forms the same probability assessment of prices rising (the same π) and the actual behaviour of prices depends on the extraneous event. For instance, if the probability of prices rising depends on high sunspot activity, then prices will rise so long as there is high sunspot activity and the bubble bursts when there is low sunspot activity. Thus sunspot activity influences the behaviour of the economy, even though it has no affect on the fundamentals, because it becomes a coordinating device for beliefs about π in the class of equilibria defined by 5.17.

In summary, the existence of multiple rational expectations equilibria cannot be lightly discounted. The general difficulty this poses for the rational expectations hypothesis is simple: How is the agent to choose between equilibria? Each satisfies the condition that when acted upon widely will only produce white noise errors, so each looks as good as the other from the vantage point of rational expectations. Something else must be introduced, like a shared belief about the influence of sunspot activity, to firm up the analysis of expectations because the rational expectations hypothesis by itself is insufficient. I shall say more later about this 'something else' and policy. For now, I wish to examine the way the multiplicity of equilibria compounds the difficulties of learning.

First, it forecloses on any argument that we can simply presume on evolutionary grounds that rational agents will eventually learn the rational expectation (and so ignore the problems in section 5.2. For instance, it is not possible to argue that, since those learning the rational expectation will prosper relative to those who do not, those holding a rational expectation will gradually displace those who do not and we do not have to worry about the learning problems in detail as evolutionary selection processes will take care of them. When there are multiple equilibria, all paths do not lead to Rome and the interaction between learners is likely to affect the selection of a rational expectation and so learning and its difficulties (as in section 5.2) cannot be ignored.

Second, the actual problem of learning has been complicated because individuals must now coordinate their expectations with others. To tease out the additional difficulty, it will be helpful to make explicit the game theoretic aspects of expectation formation in the social world.

In section 5.2, it was possible for an individual to get it 'right' independently of what other individuals thought or did. This was a contrived property of the model because I assumed the relationship in equation 5.2 determined the rate of return. In general, this will not be the case in the social world, even when there is a unique rational expectation equilibrium. The pay-off to you of holding a particular expectation will typically depend on the actions of others (and hence their expectations) and so your best expectation cannot be defined independently of the expectation entertained by others.

In effect, each individual is playing a game with others and the rational expectation is given by the Nash equilibrium in this game. (Recall from Chapter 4, the Nash equilibrium is given by strategies which form best replies to each other. Thus when individuals entertain expectations about others which correspond to the Nash strategies, they will be rational expectations because when each individual acts on these expectations they will choose the Nash strategies and thus confirm each other's expectations.) Hence, the general problem of learning can be re-expressed as the process of groping for a Nash equilibrium in a game where, for one reason or another of imperfect information about the game, it is not transparent at the outset for all agents in the economy.

Put in this way, it should become clear what additional problems arise with multiple rational expectations equilibria. When there is a unique rational expectations equilibrium (that is, a unique Nash equilibrium) it is plausible to argue along with some game theorists that, the moment the structure of the game is known and we presume common instrumental rationality and common knowledge, individuals will play Nash strategies (and entertain rational expectations). In this context, learning is strictly concerned with understanding the structure of the game. However, the moment there are multiple rational expectations equilibria (that is, multiple Nash equilibria), learning has an additional dimension. Once the structure of the game becomes known, the individual must still grope towards an understanding of how each individual will select one Nash equilibrium from among the many. This is a matter of coordinating your belief with those of others – for instance, by the use of sunspot activity in the example of speculative bubbles. By definition, this will involve learning about those things which others regard as important but which are extraneous to the game itself. Thus, we have an additional layer to the learning problem which the individual must face. Quite how the policy debate is affected by the presence of this extra layer is likely to depend on the precise extraneous information which is used for selecting an equilibrium, and I examine this in more detail in the next section.

5.4 Overlapping Generations and Bootstrap Equilibria

This section develops an overlapping generations model and it shows how the mechanisms for selecting a rational expectation equilibrium can have a crucial impact on the demand management policy debate. In turn, this suggests the possibility of a new domain of government influence operating via an ability to affect these selection mechanisms (that is, the sources of extraneous information). The model has the following attributes:

1. There are n individuals born each period, indexed by t, each individual lives for two periods, indexed by 1 and 2 (= young and old), and each

individual has a utility function that depends on consumption when young and consumption when old which he or she seeks to maximize,

$$U(C_{1t}, C_{2t}) \qquad (5.18)$$

where C is the consumption of the only commodity.

2. The individual is endowed with some of this commodity in each period, the commodity is perishable and the individual can transfer purchasing power between the first and second period by purchasing money. Thus the individual maximizes 5.18 subject to the following constraints

$$C_1 + M_t/P_t = E_1$$

and

$$C_2 = M_t/P_{t+1} + E_2 \qquad (5.19)$$

where P is the price of the only good and E is the endowment in each period.

3. For simplicity I shall assume that all individuals are identical with respect to utility functions and endowments, so that the competitive equilibrium in the economy can be studied, when it involves exchange, as an exchange between two individuals of different generations (that is, between a 'young' and an 'old' person) under conditions where each individual accepts the price vector as given.

To study the competitive equilibrium in this economy, it is convenient to derive a typical 'young' person's offer curve, that is his or her demand for money which he or she will demand in exchange for not consuming a part of his or her endowment in that period. Figure 5.1 helps because it captures the essentials of a two-period utility maximizing decision.

First, it can be noted from this that a positive offer (that is, $C_1 < E_1$) depends on a particular conjunction of budget constraint and preferences. As it is drawn, this condition is satisfied, but it would not be difficult to imagine a different configuration where this condition was not satisfied. When the condition is not satisfied the individual would like to borrow rather than save and there is a negative demand for money. However, there is no incentive for the older individual to oblige the 'young' by consuming less than their endowment in that period, so the exchange between generations will not occur. In these circumstances, it is easy to derive the equilibrium for the economy: it is characterized by each generation simply consuming their endowment in each period.

Figure 5.1 Intertemporal choice

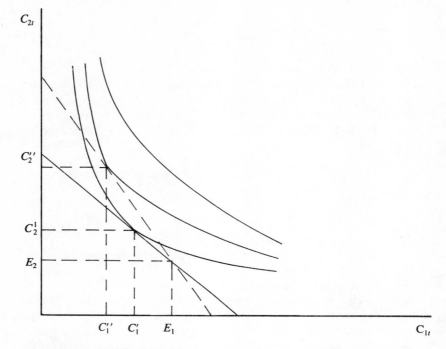

I shall focus hereafter only on conjunctions of endowments, prices and preferences which satisfy the condition of yielding a positive offer of commodities for money, with the result that the equilibrium is characterized by an exchange between generations. In the construction of these equilibria, it is helpful to note that consumption in each period depends on relative prices and as P_{t+1}/P_t falls, so C_2 rises but the effects on C_1 are unclear because the income and substitution effects operate in opposite directions. As I have drawn it the substitution effect dominates, but it is possible that the reverse will hold with the result that C_1 increases and offers $(E-C)$ decrease. Figure 5.2 depicts these offers, for a given expected future price, $P^{e'}_{t+1}$, as a function of P_t. It allows for the possibility that as P_t increases beyond some point the substitution effects get swamped by income effects with the result that the offer curve bends backward.

The real money supply is also drawn on this diagram as a function of price level by assuming a constant nominal money supply. This is what the 'old' generation offer the 'young' in return for commodities: it represents demand for the commodity. Thus a market equilibrium will occur when there is a price which equates one offer with the other. When the offer curve bends back

Figure 5.2   Trades between generations

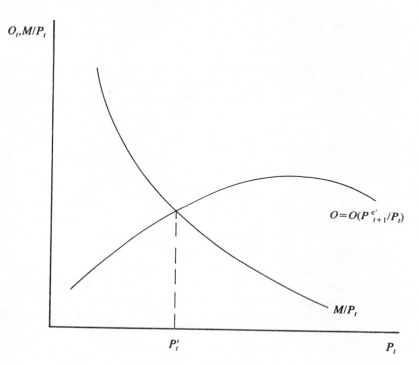

sufficiently, there will be more than one price where this condition is met, but for the moment I shall confine myself to cases where the equilibrium is on the 'normal' part of the offer curve.

A competitive equilibrium for such an economy will be given by a vector of prices stretching into the future, $(P_t, P_{t+1}, P_{t+2} \ldots)$, such that for each time period the demand for the commodity by the 'old' equals its supply by the 'young'. Through inspection of Figure 5.2, it will be clear that there are an infinite continuum of such price vectors. I can produce any equilibrium price in t through suitable changes in the expected future price because these changes will shift the offer curve into whatever is the desired location for this price to be an equilibrium. Furthermore, given the recursive structure of the model, it is plain that any price expectation for $t+1$ can be turned into a rational expectation, that is, equal to the price of that period, with a suitable choice of the expected price in $t+2$ so as to manipulate the location for the offer curve in $t+1$ into a position which will generate the equilibrium price in $t+1$ which had been expected in t, and so on for each period. Whatever price I start with in t, I can work forward and write in the subsequent set of prices which, if expected, will equilibrate demand and supply in each time period. In short, there are an infinite continuum of rational expectations equilibria in this model.

The general properties of these equilibria are discussed in the next section. For now, I want to make some specific observations about particular equilibrium selection mechanisms.

As it stands, the model is incomplete without some explanation of how one equilibrium comes to be selected: we need some way to fix either the current price or the expected future price(s). Once one has been determined then the other can be calculated as part of the construction of the rational expectations equilibrium. I shall consider two particular possibilities here because they connect directly with the policy debate over activism.

First, to set the scene, assume the price is initially determined at P'_t (somehow) and there is an increase in the supply of money which is given to the 'old' generation. The 'old' and 'young' are both told about this increase in the period in which it occurs and they are able to reset prices accordingly. So, the increase had not been previously anticipated, but in the time period in which it occurs it is effectively anticipated because all agents are free to take it into account in resetting prices.

The question is: What will happen to prices in the current period? We know from the above that there are infinite continuum of rational expectations equilibria associated with the new money supply and the issue is: How is one selected? One way to settle this question is to assume that individuals hold certain extraneous beliefs which enable them to select an equilibrium. For instance, suppose the individuals hold 'monetarists/NCM' beliefs and so believe that current prices will rise equiproportionately to the increase in the money supply. In these circumstances, the 'monetarist/NCM' belief selects the equilibrium. It selects the one which confirms that belief. Accordingly, we have prices increasing to P''_t as this restores the real supply of money to its original value. For this to be an equilibrium, the offer curve must shift out to the new location in Figure 5.3 and this is achieved when expectations of future prices rise to $P^{e''}_{t+1}$. How much is this necessary rise in future prices? Since individual's offers depend only on relative prices and the same level of real offers as before is required (given that the real supply of money will not change when current prices rise at the same rate as the money supply) then future prices must rise at the same rate as current prices to leave relative prices unchanged. Thus, individuals, guided by 'monetarist/NCM' beliefs, expect future prices to rise at the same rate as the money supply and this means current prices will rise at the same rate. Hence, we obtain the result that the increase in the money supply leaves the level of offers unchanged and all that happens is that current and future prices rise at the rate of increase in the money supply. In short, the 'monetarist/NCM' beliefs are confirmed for the simple reason that they have been used as a species of extraneous information to select the equilibrium for the economy.

Figure 5.3 'NCM' bootstraps

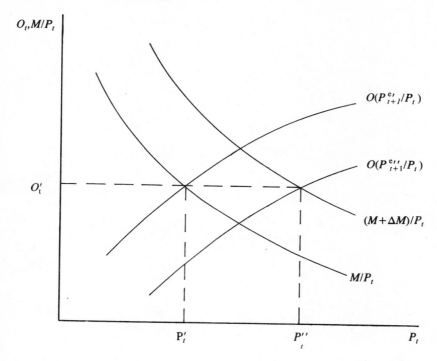

Alternatively, imagine individuals hold Keynesian extraneous beliefs. To be specific, individuals now hold extraneous beliefs to the effect that a change in the money supply has no influence on current prices, it only alters real variables (a rough Keynesian belief!). This helps each individual to select the expectation for future prices because the belief is only consistent with a fall in expected price which shifts the offer curve in the direction indicated in Figure 5.4. Hence individuals guided by these beliefs expect that future prices will fall and will act according to the new offer curve to produce no change in the equilibrium current price. Only current offers (that is, real variables) change, rising to O''. Again, the beliefs are confirmed.

To put a little more realism into this overlapping generations model, let the endowment be labour which can be used to produce the consumption commodity via a linear production function ($E=L=C$). It is now a model of production as well as exchange and the 'offer' by the young in exchange for money is to supply labour to the 'old' who use it for (public as opposed to private) production of the commodity. Thus, with the Keynesian extraneous beliefs doing the selecting, we observe that the increase in the money supply produces

Figure 5.4 '*Keynesian' bootstraps*

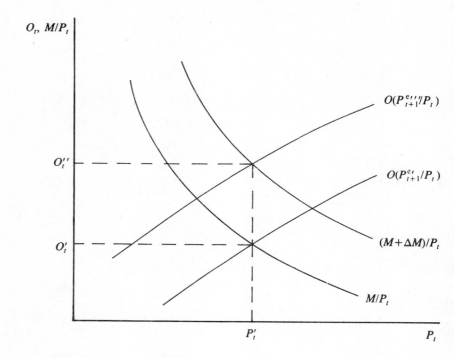

a rise in employment and (public) output.

A second possible way of determining future expectations, and thereby selecting the equilibrium, is via 'animal spirits'. Suppose there is a surge of optimism about the future which translates into the belief that prices in the future will be lower than had previously been expected. The offer curve will shift out as in Figure 5.4 and for a given money supply we will observe a fall in current prices as well as an increase in current offers (that is, output and employment). 'Animal spirits' is, of course, a kind of free-floating equilibrium selection device. The point of introducing it is simply to show that it is possible to make sense of the claim that 'animal spirits' drive the economy. (Broadly speaking, this is one of the claims of Keynes and it makes perfect sense in this model.)

Of course, these reflections on potential selection mechanisms would not count for much in the discussion of policy if there were not clear welfare differences between equilibria. But, whenever the choice of equilibrium involves real changes there will be some welfare effects and so the issue assumes significance. Indeed, it can be noted that in the example where an increase in the money supply took place under Keynesian beliefs, the new equilibrium is a pareto improvement over the old one as far as the two generations are concerned. The 'old' generation is plainly better-off, and with a fall in the future price, Figure 5.1 reveals that the 'young' are also better-off.

In conclusion, this brief discussion of equilibrium selection is important for the policy debate in three interrelated ways. First, it suggests that the issue of activism in demand management could turn, in part, on the 'theoretical' beliefs of the private sector (that is, when these beliefs are the extraneous information which enable equilibrium selection). The case for 'hands-off' is strengthened when the private sector holds 'monetarist/NCM' beliefs because changes in the money supply have no real effect. Whereas the case for activism is improved by the 'fact' that a change in the money supply has real effects which can be welfare improving for both generations when the private sector holds Keynesian-type beliefs. Second, some care is required in using such 'facts' to test the theoretical beliefs of the private sector. Indeed, in these circumstances, it would not make any sense to use the behaviour of the economy as some independent test of the theories because the beliefs are self-fulfilling.

Third, and more generally, if governments are concerned with economic outcomes, then they not only have to pay attention to the extraneous beliefs held by the private sector, they may also wish to influence those beliefs. I have focused on two types of theoretical belief because of their connections with the debate over activism. But plainly, the beliefs that the private sector take to be relevant for economic outcomes may be much wider than this and they constitute a new and potentially fruitful arena for government policy attention.

5.5 Cycles, Sunspots Equilibria and Permanent Recessions

To study the equilibria in this overlapping generations model in more detail, it is convenient to represent the offer curve in a slightly different manner. This is done in Figure 5.5. Here I plot the various combinations of offers for each time period made by a particular generation as the relative price between time periods changes. The vertical axis plots the negative of the offer ($O = E - C$) in the second period: this will be a positive number because with trade between generations the individual consumes more than his or her endowment in the second period and so the actual offer ($E - C$) is negative. It will equal the offer in equilibrium of the young from the next generation (O_{1t+1}). As the relative price of future consumption falls, one moves out along the locus. Consequently, future consumption is always rising but current consumption may rise or fall depending on the interplay between income and substitution effects. Figure 5.5 depicts a case where the substitution effects dominate. When the income effects dominate, the locus starts to bend back on itself. This possibility is captured in Figure 5.6.

Figure 5.5   Saddlepoint equilibrium in overlapping generations

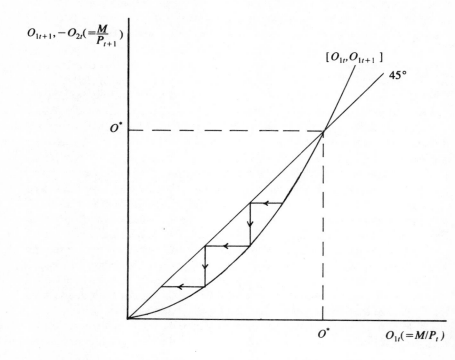

In a competitive equilibrium, we know that these offers must be equal to the real supply of money in each period. Thus, I can discover the properties of a stationary equilibrium (where prices are the same in each period, and each generation merely replicates the behaviour of the previous generation) by introducing a 45 degree line. In Figure 5.5 there are two steady-state equilibria, O^* and the origin. The latter is the case where no trade takes place between generations and the price of money goes to zero. The other, O^*, is an unstable equilibrium and so, provided there were good reasons for discounting the explosive price behaviour implied by any other path for prices, it would command our attention as a unique equilibrium solution for prices. This, in turn, would cast doubt on the relevance of the multiplicity of equilibria discussed in the previous section because they would have to belong to these explosive paths. However, it will be recalled from section 5.3 that these explosive paths cannot be so easily dismissed, especially once probabilistic, sunspot driven, bubbles are admitted. So, the general problem of multiple equilibria remains even in this case and the discussion in section 5.4 remains potentially relevant.

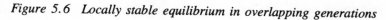

Figure 5.6 Locally stable equilibrium in overlapping generations

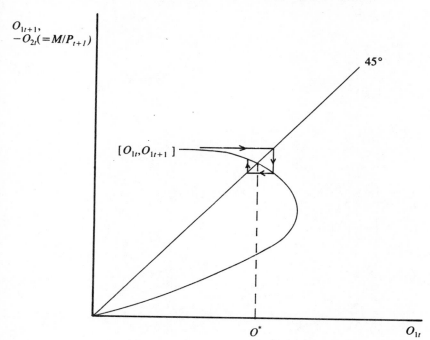

Figure 5.6 illustrates a case where there is a locally stable stationary state at O^*. The condition for local stability is simply that the absolute value of the slope of locus at the intersection with the 45-degree line be greater than 1. It is an important possibility because local stability means that there are an infinite number of possible paths for prices. Hence, in this instance, it is not necessary to introduce the arguments about explosive paths to preserve the insights concerning multiplicity in section 5.4. In fact, a consideration of this case also yields a number of further insights. I shall focus on three.

First, it is possible to obtain cyclical and more generally chaotic equilibrium solutions for prices and offers. To appreciate this, examine Figure 5.7. I have drawn this so that there is a three-point cycle, from O_1 to O_2 to O_3 and then back to O_1 and so on.

The significance of this demonstration is that reasonably plausible models have been constructed with the property of a three-point cycle and there is a theorem, Sarkovsky's theorem, which shows that any process generating a three-point cycle will also generate cycles of every order. Thus, once a three-point cycle has been shown, we know that the process is also capable of much

Figure 5.7   Three point cycle in overlapping generations

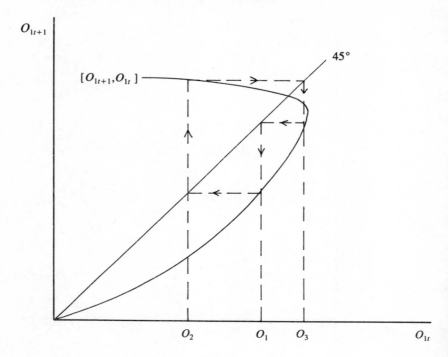

more complicated, chaotic, behaviour. This means that these models contain an alternative explanation of the business cycle: they are an endogenous property of some of the many rational expectations equilibria.

Second, a range of sunspots equilibria may also feature in the set of equilibria. Suppose there are two possible outcomes, O' and O'' (associated with P' and P'' such that $O' < O^* < O''$), and there is an extraneous event that takes on two values and upon which individuals condition their expectation of either O' or O'' being the future equilibrium. I shall assume that the following Markov stationary matrix defines the transition probabilities for the extraneous event

next period

		O'	O''
this period	O'	q'	$1-q'$
	O''	$1-q''$	q''

and thus the individual's probability assessment of O' being followed by O' or O'' and the probability assessment of O'' being followed by O' or O''.

With these beliefs, O' and O'' will be the two equilibria which we observe depending on the behaviour of the extraneous event, provided $O'(P')$ and $O''(P'')$ satisfy the first order conditions for maximizing 5.18 in these new circumstances. To explore this in more detail I shall assume that 5.18 is separable into U and V functions for first and second period consumption. Thus, given the uncertainty about the future price level, the maximization problem becomes

$$\max \ U(C_1) + EV(C_2) \tag{5.20}$$

With the equilibrium O', this means that the following first order condition would have to be satisfied

$$[U'\,(E_1 - M/P')]/P' = q'\{[V'\,(E_2 + M/P')]/P'\} + \\ (1 - q')\{[V'(E_2 + M/P'')]/P''\} \tag{5.21}$$

This simply means that for P' to be an equilibrium this period with either P' or P'' as the possible equilibria next period, it entails that, given the beliefs about likely prices next period, the marginal utility of expenditure must be equal to the expected marginal utility of expenditure next period. Likewise for the equilibrium O'', there is an analogous first order condition that must be satisfied

$$[U'\,(E_1 - M/P'')]/P'' = q''\{[V'\,(E_2 + M/P'')]/P''\} + \\ (1 - q'')\{[V'(E_2 + M/P')]/P'\} \tag{5.22}$$

When a set (q',q'',P',P'') satisfy 5.21 and 5.22, we have a sunspots equilibria, since what we have demonstrated is that P' can satisfy the first order conditions for maximization given the particular beliefs about P' and P'' in the future and likewise P'' can also satisfy the first order conditions given those beliefs. Thus P' and P'' are both consistent with those beliefs and the occurrence of one or the other depends on the behaviour of the extraneous event which conditions those beliefs in the Markov matrix. Since, there are two equations which have to be satisfied and four degrees of freedom over the choice of (q',q'',P',P''), it is likely that there will be sunspots equilibria of this sort.

Third, it is possible to note that the Markov matrix of transition probabilities may produce a convergence of the economy towards one of these states rather than the other. When either q' or q'' is non-zero, but close to zero, the economy will converge asymptotically towards one state or the other. In short, the economy will move towards a state of permanent recession or boom.

5.6 Conclusion

This chapter has focused on the difficulties with the rational expectations hypothesis as used by the NCM in its argument against policy activism. There are two principle problems. One relates to the difficulties of learning a rational expectation even when there is a unique rational expectations equilibrium. The potential lack of convergence means that expectations will be better captured by the learning procedure than the rational expectations hypothesis. And this has implications for the demand management debate because many learning procedures will approximate something like an adaptive expectations scheme.

The second problem arises when there are multiple rational expectations equilibria. To put it bluntly, the likely existence of multiple equilibria makes the rational expectations hypothesis incomplete as a theory of expectation formation. Something must be added to explain how one rational expectation is selected. Formally, individuals have to coordinate their beliefs by using some shared piece of extraneous information.

This reliance on extraneous information connects directly with the policy debate when the extraneous information used to select an equilibrium is economic theories. For instance, we found that demand management activism affects the real side of the economy when individuals hold Keynesian beliefs, while it only affects prices when individuals hold monetarist/NCM beliefs – thus qualifying the NCM impotency result in Chapter 4.

More generally, the role played by extraneous information points to a new domain for government policy: policy might be directed at influencing the sources of extraneous information used by individuals. After all, the welfare properties of the various equilibria are likely to be very different (witness the possibility of permanent recession in the last section); and so the selection of equilibrium is likely to be a matter of some importance and concern to policymakers. As yet, we do not have much to say about the sources of extraneous belief and what might be involved in this new policy domain. Nevertheless, it may have more than a hint of Orwell's 1984 about it; and this is worth dispelling.

To say that the governments might want to influence private-sector belief formation can sound vey much like Orwell's 1984. This is a salutary reminder but it is also misleading. To tease out what is wrong with the Orwellian gloss, it may be helpful to introduce a distinction between beliefs which hold contingently because other people hold the belief and those beliefs which hold independently of what others think for 'substantive' reasons. The charge of Orwell's 1984 sticks when the beliefs fall into the latter category. But, this is not the case with the choice between monetarist/NCM and Keynesian beliefs in the model put forward in section 5.5.

Monetarist/NCM and Keynesian beliefs only work for the individual in that model, in the sense of generating a rational expectation, when the same belief is held by other individuals. The beliefs have no intrinsic virtue as far as forming a rational expectation is concerned. They become contingently useful when others hold the belief because when the belief is shared it becomes a coordinating device for the selection of an equilibrium from the multiplicity.

Thus, when we talk about governments influencing beliefs we are not talking about an Orwellian world. Instead, we are opening up the possibility of the government being concerned with shifting society from one coordinating device to another because the switch produces a superior outcome and because it is difficult for individuals acting in isolation to change a coordinating convention by themselves.

As a final word, perhaps, it should be emphasized that the rediscovery of efficacious Keynesian activism (either because individuals are always learning using something like adaptive expectations or because they hold Keynesian beliefs) and the discovery of a new arena for government action has not entailed a departure from either of the hallmark assumptions of the NCM. I have assumed competitive microfoundations with market clearing prices and a desire to hold rational expectations throughout. The policy conclusions are rather less clear cut than they were at the end of Chapter 4 simply because there is more to the formation of rational expectations than the early NCM led us to believe.

5.7 Brief Notes on the Literature

The discussion of information transmission and learning comes from Bray (1985); this contains references to a number of her own papers which have been concerned with learning and convergence. Grossman and Stiglitz (1980) provide an earlier discussion with a variety of comparative static insights over the degree of information transmission. Friedman (1979) gives an early argument connecting learning with adaptive expectations and Frydman and Phelps (1983) contains a general discussion of learning problems. Bubbles emerge as a possibility in Azariadis (1981) and are discussed further in Blanchard and Watson (1982). There is a growing literature on overlapping generations models: Samuelson (1958) is the landmark contribution in English and Azariadis (1981) contains many of the central 'modern' insights, especially with respect to sunspots equilibria. Geanakoplos (1987) provides a useful survey of the literature and Geanakoplos and Polemarchakis (1986) are the specific source for the discussion of bootstraps and animal spirits in the fourth section. Hahn (1980) gives an earlier example of the bootstrap phenomenon and Grandmont (1985) is the source for models with chaotic behaviour.

6. The New Keynesian Macroeconomics II: Price Determination

6.1 Introduction

A variety of imperfectly competitive microfoundations for macroeconomics are presented in this and the next chapter. These alternatives to the competitive model of social interaction, used by the NCM, offer several possible explanations of nominal and real price and wage stickiness. It will be recalled from Chapter 3 that it is the failure of nominal wages and prices to adjust to a change in nominal demand which needs to be explained for the occurrence of Keynesian as opposed to Classical unemployment; and that the speed of adjustment of wages and prices was a crucial variable in the summary of policy debate over demand management activism contained in sections 2.3, 2.5 and 3.5. Consequently, these explanations of nominal wage and price stickiness lend support to the Keynesian explanation of, and demand management prescription for, unemployment. To reinforce those early observations concerning importance of price stickiness in this debate, this chapter begins by formally introducing the possibility of some gradual price adjustment into the canonical NCM model (that is, the one which was first used to demonstrate the policy impotence proposition in section 4.2). Once price stickiness is introduced into that model, the policy impotence/neutrality proposition collapses.

Sections 6.3 and 6.4 introduce the equivalent canonical NKM model of price stickiness. It has many of the features of the NCM models, for instance the reliance on representative agents, but it studies price-setting behaviour under monopolistic competition when there are small menu costs associated with price changes. The model serves to introduce a general NKM argument on this issue: one which turns on the recognition that individual decisions often have important spillover effects for other individuals; and which notes that, in the presence of such spillovers, the uncoordinated pursuit of self-interest can produce collectively self-defeating outcomes. This will sound like an old and familiar argument about market failure when there are externalities. And it is, but it has been given new life by the NKM in this macro debate.

Section 6.5 presents a model where aggregate price stickiness emerges because price setting by individual firms is staggered. In this model, as in the small menu costs one of sections 6.3 and 6.4, it is the presence of information difficulties of one kind or another which play a crucial role in the explanation. Section 6.6 reinforces this observation with a discussion of the importance of 'trust' which can lead firms and individuals to rely on conventions – or, to echo the terminology of Chapter 5, to rely on 'shared sources of extraneous information'. Conventions of this sort can serve economic agents well (and so are perfectly rational to follow) but they are not always fine-tuned enough to produce the instantaneous price adjustments which might mitigate unemployment.

The NKM has tended to emphasize the role of nominal price stickiness over wage stickiness. This is perhaps an understandable reaction to the Classical and NCM preoccupation with the real wage rate, and it explains the ordering of these last two chapters. Nevertheless, it should not blind us to the important connections between wage and price formation. To appreciate these connections at the outset and to avoid the potential for confusion in this area, it will be helpful to introduce an important distinction between real and nominal rigidity.

Nominal wage and price rigidity refers to the failure of agents to adjust the nominal wage or nominal price in response to a change in nominal demand, whereas real wage and price rigidity refers to the failure of agents to adjust the relative price or the real wage rate when there is a real shock. It is tempting to elide one sort of explanation with another, but this is a mistake because real price/wage rigidity need not entail nominal price/wage rigidity. In particular, indexing all prices to changes in nominal demand within the economy will preserve all real prices/wages whilst enabling perfect adjustments in nominal wages and prices to changes in demand. Thus, explanations of real wage and price rigidity cannot automatically be put to the service of explaining nominal rigidities. However, there is a way in which real rigidities help explain nominal rigidities in the NKM literature.

When individuals have doubts about whether all agents will adjust to a nominal demand shock, the nominal shock will appear to the individual agent as a real shock and so any source of real rigidity will now help to explain why the individual agent does not adjust the price or wage. This mechanism connecting real with nominal wage and price stickiness highlights the coordination aspects of wage and price changes because the individual incentive to change price or wage in response to a nominal demand shock rises as the number of other actors in the economy adjust (or are expected to adjust) their prices/wages. Thus some degree of real stickiness may forestall price and wage adjustment when few are expected to adjust but it will not prevent adjustment if many are expected to adjust and so the issue of coordination arises. In fact, there are many aspects to wage and price setting which involve solving coordination games, and the general message is that while conventions might be expected to emerge to facilitate coordination, there is no guarantee that we will be using the best convention for all contingencies.

As a final word in this introduction, it is perhaps worth noting that nominal price stickiness is not only central to the policy debate, it also provides a ready explanation of why output movements are serially correlated. In the absence of any compensating manipulation of aggregate demand, the adjustment of prices to a demand shock is spread out over a number of time periods and so output systematically deviates from the 'natural' or NAIRU value during this period of adjustment. This is, of course, really just the other side of the policy potence proposition since it is the long drawn out period of output adjustment which provides the opportunity for an effective manipulation of aggregate demand by the government.

6.2 Sticky Prices in the Canonical NCM Model

Let us return to the aggregate supply function in the NCM model (equation 4.2). I shall denote the price level that satisfies this equation as p^* and I interpret it as the equilibrium price level agents would like to see given price expectations and output levels. Thus,

$$y_t = y^* + a_0[p_t^* - p_t^e] + u_{1t} \tag{6.1}$$

I introduce this interpretation because I want to allow for the possibility that actual prices only gradually adjust to this equilibrium value, as in

$$p_t - p_{t-1} = \beta(p_t^* - p_{t-1}) \tag{6.2}$$

Naturally, this type of stickiness is what needs to be explained but, for the moment, I shall accept that it exists in order to explore its implications for the conduct of aggregate demand policies. Finally, I shall collapse the aggregate demand side of the economy, previously equations 4.3 and 4.4, into a single equation because this simplifies the algebra, as in

$$y_t = \gamma(m_t - p_t) + \delta g_t + u_{2t} \tag{6.3}$$

When I solve these three equations for p, I obtain

$$p_t = [\alpha\beta\gamma m_t + \alpha\beta\delta g_t - \alpha\beta y^* + \beta p_t^e + (1-\beta)p_{t-1} + \alpha\beta(u_{1t} + u_{2t})] / (1+\alpha\beta\gamma) \tag{6.4}$$

where $\alpha = (1/a_0)$.

This reduced form can now be used to solve for the rational expectation of p, as in

$$p_t^e = [\alpha\beta\gamma m_t^e + \alpha\beta\delta g_t^e - \alpha\beta y^* - (1-\beta)p_t]/(1+\alpha\beta\gamma-\beta) \quad (6.5)$$

To see what this implies for the behaviour of y, substitute 6.5 into 6.1 and 6.2 and solve with 6.3 for y,

$$y_t = (\gamma m_t + \delta g_t)/(1+\alpha\beta\gamma) - (\alpha\beta^2\gamma^2 m_t^e + \alpha\beta^2\gamma\delta g_t^e)$$
$$/[(1+\alpha\beta\gamma)(1+\alpha\beta\gamma-\beta)] + [\alpha\beta\gamma y^* - (1-\beta)\gamma p_{t-1}]$$
$$/(1+\alpha\beta\gamma-\beta) + (u_{2t} + \alpha\beta\gamma u_{1t})/(1+\alpha\beta\gamma) \quad (6.6)$$

An inspection of 6.6 makes plain that the policy stance of the government will influence the level of output, even when monetary policy and fiscal policy changes are perfectly anticipated (so that $m=m^e$ and $g=g^e$). Furthermore, it is easy to check that it is the introduction of price stickiness which has produced the result: let the adjustment parameter in 6.2 (β) equal 1 so that $p_t=p_t^*$; and equation 6.6 loses all terms in anticipated money and fiscal policy and so restores the policy impotence/neutrality proposition.

The algebra of this may be clear, but it is worth pausing to recover the intuitions. Essentially, they are the same as those discussed in section 3.5. Agents form rational expectations about the price level, but in doing this they take account of the gradual price adjustment. Thus, they recognize that prices do not adjust completely to the intersection of the conventional aggregate supply and demand functions and form their expectations accordingly. Once prices no longer move to equate aggregate demand and supply, we need some theory of output determination because traditionally the intersection of aggregate demand and supply functions gives us both prices and output. By construction in this model, we have allowed output to be determined by aggregate demand by using the same symbol for both. This, of course, is the natural interpretation for Keynesians to make and helps to explain the emergence of the Keynesian results. In effect, the failure of prices to adjust, forces agents to trade at false prices. They recognize this and so rational expectations are not being confounded. Yet the way is open to government demand management because the constraints which agents know they will encounter when they trade at false prices can be relaxed through the judicious manipulation of demand. Indeed, the introduction of rational expectations here is likely to be a bonus since it means agents will quickly revise their expectations regarding the constraints which they face in markets.

This is an important result which makes it all the more pressing to discover whether there are plausible reasons for supposing that prices might be slow to adjust to their equilibrium values. Before turning to this issue, though, there is Dornbusch's (1976) development of a sticky price version of the NCM model which is worth briefly mentioning. It is interesting because it contributes to an understanding of the exchange rate volatility we have experienced under the regime of floating rates since 1973.

Assume the economy operates in a world of perfect capital mobility and risk neutrality; so that arbitrage ensures that the expected returns from holding home country treasury bills and foreign ones must be the same. Further, suppose that with a full adjustment of prices the economy exhibits money neutrality with the exchange rate following the path predicted by purchasing power parity (that is, all prices change in the same proportion as the change in the money supply, including the price of foreign currency which is given by the exchange rate). Finally, assume that while final commodity prices only adjust gradually, the exchange rate and the interest rate move so as to equilibrate the foreign exchange and domestic money markets at all times. Now, consider a sudden increase in the home money supply which is accompanied by only a partial adjustment of all domestic final commodity prices. This means the real supply of money increases and so the instantaneous domestic money market equilibrium will entail a fall in home interest rates. However, if domestic interest rates fall, the return from holding domestic treasury bills falls and this will provoke outward movement of capital, thus placing downward pressure on the exchange rate.

When will the exchange stop falling? When the expected returns from holding foreign and home treasury bills are again equalized. But with home interest rates at a lower value, this is only possible when there is an expectation that the exchange rate will appreciate (thus reducing the home currency return from holding a foreign treasury bill in line with the lower return on home treasury bills). Recall we are in a world of rational expectations, so this expectation can only be entertained if the actual time path of exchange rates shows an appreciation. Hence the exchange rate now must instantaneously move to a level which will enable it to follow the suitable path of appreciation – that is, it must drop below its long-run equilibrium value.

What does this imply for the behaviour of exchange rates? It follows from the assumption of long-run neutrality that once prices have adjusted there will be a depreciation which matches the increase in the money supply. Accordingly, we will observe an instantaneous excessive depreciation of the exchange rate, relative to what is required in the long run, as this will create the expectation of an appreciation which is necessary when, with international arbitrage during the period of gradual price adjustment, domestic interest rates are below world levels. In other words, price stickiness in one part of the economy produces excessive volatility in a part (foreign exchange markets) where prices are free to adjust!

6.3 The NKM Insight: Small Menu Costs and Spillovers

The essence of this NKM explanation of price stickiness is that small costs of adjusting prices can forestall price changes because the failure to adjust prices only involves second-order losses. The point can be appreciated if we use a Taylor's expansion of a firm's profit function $\pi(P)$. Let us define P^* as the profit maximizing price and P as the price which is actually charged, then the loss from not adjusting the price to the profit maximizing level can be approximated by

$$\pi(P^*) - \pi(P) = \pi'(P^*)(P^*-P) - 1/2\pi''(P^*)(P^*-P)^2 \qquad (6.7)$$

Since P^* maximizes profits, it follows $\pi'(P^*)=0$ when firms set price. Hence, the first term here goes to zero and the profit loss is second order as it depends on the square of $(P^* - P)$. The same point can be seen diagrammatically in Figure 6.1 by considering the monopolist operating with constant costs. P^* is the profit maximizing price once demand has moved to its new location (DD) and P_O is the old price charged by the monopolist before the shift. There are two effects on profits if the firm does not adjust price: there is a gain of area A and a loss of area B. Consequently, the overall effect is a 'second-order' magnitude: it is the net effect of this 'push and pull' in opposite directions ($=B-A$).

Figure 6.1 Small gains from price adjustment

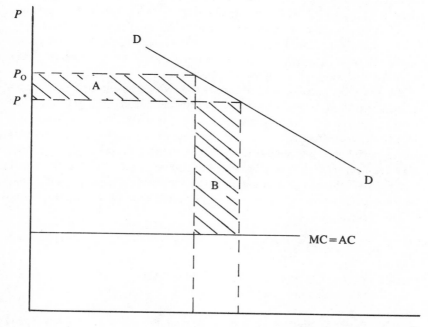

Thus when prices only deviate slightly from their profit maximizing level, the losses from non-adjustment are small and these losses will not warrant a price adjustment if there are small 'menu' costs associated with such adjustments. This insight goes some way to explaining why prices do not move to exhaust all potentially mutually beneficial trades. However, it does not fully answer the charge made by the NCM (in section 4.2) that we do not find significant numbers of £10 notes on the pavements. It would seem that we should only expect second-order welfare losses as a result of this non-adjustment. In other words, at best, it might explain why we find the odd penny on the pavement!

This is where the idea of spillovers or externalities enters the argument. When a firm decides not to change its price, it takes into account how a price change will affect its relative price and perceives only second-order gains. But this calculation ignores the contribution that price changes make to the general level of prices and thus the real supply of money and hence the level of aggregate demand and the location of individual demand curves. To be specific, consider a firm facing a fall in nominal demand because the real money supply has declined. The demand for its product, like those throughout the economy, shifts in towards the origin. The firm can change its relative price and move down this demand curve, but the second-order gains from this manoeuvre do not outweigh the menu costs and so the price is not adjusted. Yet, if all firms adjusted their prices downwards, the real supply of money would increase and the demand curve facing each firm would shift out. The problem is that, in the absence of some mechanism to capture these spillover effects, the macro impact of everyone changing prices does not enter into each individual firm's calculation of the benefits of price adjustment.

This is a classic example of an externality where the social costs of non-adjustment exceed the private ones; and it provides a ready answer to the NCM presumption that self-inteest will yield competitive market clearing prices. The NKM reminds us that the dictates of self-interest often produce collectively self-defeating outcomes when there are externalities. Or to put it differently, there are £10 notes on the pavement, but it takes a collective effort to pick them up when there are externalities. So, in the absence of a collective effort, we should not be surprised to observe the equivalent of those £10 notes – unemployment.

6.4   The Canonical NKM Model

The following assumptions are typical of the NKM models which are used to explore the consequences of small menu costs and spillovers.

1.   There are N individuals, each with identical utility functions which depend

on the consumption of each of the J commodities and the amount of labour supplied, as in

$$U = (1/\theta)[(1/J)\Sigma(JC^{\phi}_j)]^{\theta/\phi} - L \qquad (6.8)$$

2. Each individual, i, maximizes his or her utility function subject to the constraint that the sum of expenditures equals his or her share of the money stock, as in

$$M_i = \Sigma_j C_{ij} P_j \qquad (6.9)$$

This is a cash-in-advance constraint and simply helps to get money into the demand functions without making money an explicit argument in the utility function. One can imagine that individuals borrow money from the bank in anticipation of wage and profit income flows and this is repaid at the end of the period.
3. There are J firms each producing one of the J commodities under identical conditions, of constant returns to scale and diminishing marginal returns to each factor. In the short run the capital stock is fixed and the short-run production function is given by

$$Y = [\beta/\gamma L]^{1/\beta} \qquad (6.10)$$

where $\beta > 1$.

The maximization of 6.8 subject to 6.9 yields individual i's demand functions for each commodity j given by

$$Y_{ij} = (1/J)(P_j/P)^{-\alpha}(M_i/P) \qquad (6.11)$$

and a labour supply function given by

$$L_i = (W/P)^{\theta/1-\theta} \qquad (6.12)$$

where $\alpha = 1/(1-\phi)$ and P is an index of general prices

$$[(1/J)\Sigma_j (P_j)^{1-\alpha}]^{1/(1-\alpha)}$$

Thus the market demand for commodity j is given by

$$Y_j = (1/J)(P_j/P)^{-\alpha}(M/P) \qquad (6.13)$$

where M is the total money stock for the economy. In other words, demand depends on relative price, with a constant elasticity, and on the real money supply. When firm j maximizes profits subject to the constraint of this demand function, the choice of price is given by

$$P_j/P = \{\alpha\gamma[1/(\alpha-1)](W/P)(M/JP)^{\beta-1}\}^{1/(\alpha\beta-\alpha+1)} \qquad (6.14)$$

Several things are worth noting about 6.14. It will only produce meaningful results when α exceeds one; otherwise it means the constant elasticity of demand is less than one and the firm would want to choose an infinite price. Of more importance, perhaps, it will be recalled that all firms are identical here and so it follows that the choice of relative price (P_j/P) must be the same for all firms in equilibrium. But, if prices are identical then, since P is an index of all prices, it follows that the ratio P_j/P must be equal to 1 in this symmetric equilibrium. Consequently, the equilibrium price P^* is given by

$$P^* = \{(\alpha-1)/[(W^*/P^*)\alpha\gamma]\}^{1/(1-\beta)} M/J \qquad (6.15)$$

Finally, the equilibrium wage rate is obtained by equating labour demand with labour supply. When $P_j/P = 1$, it is

$$W^*/P^* = \{[J\gamma/N\beta][(M)/(JP^*)]^{\beta}\}^{(1-\theta)/\theta} \qquad (6.16)$$

The model can now be used to elaborate the NKM argument sketched in section 6.3. Consider a reduction in the money supply. Inspection of equations 6.14 to 6.16 reveals that the economy exhibits the property of money neutrality – both equations 6.15 and 6.16 are homogenous of degree 1 in $[W, P$ and $M]$ and equation 6.13 is homogenous of degree 0 in $[P$ and $M]$. So, we know that in equilibrium the reduction in the money supply will be associated with an equiproportionate change in all wages and prices. Furthermore, we can see the mechanism which prompts these changes in prices. From 6.14, all firms want to reduce their relative price after the fall in the money supply and the only way available to them for doing this is to drop their own price. In the aggregate, as all firms do this, the general level of prices falls and this leads to an increase in the real supply of money. The real supply of money continues to rise as long as firms wish to cut prices and they will want to cut prices so long as the real supply of money is below its original equilibrium value. Accordingly, prices fall until the real supply of money has been restored to its original value. Once this has been achieved, and with all firms still charging the same relative price, the quantities of each commodity which are demanded and supplied are restored to their original equilibrium values. *Voila!* The change in the money supply has no effect on the real side of the economy, it simply causes an equiproportionate change in all prices and wages.

The crux of the NKM argument now is simple: it is, that this adjustment process can be forestalled when there are small menu costs. (I shall say something more about these menu costs in a moment, for now, let us accept that they exist.) We know from the earlier argument that gains from price adjustments are second order and consequently these gains can be outweighed by relatively small menu costs, with the result that the adjustment process of prices may never get off the ground.

The argument is simple enough. Nevertheless, it requires careful elaboration because there appear to be some obvious weak links. In particular, why is there only a consideration of the costs of price adjustment? Surely, there are costs associated with quantity adjustments and they must be bought into the picture before we can pretend to have an explanation of why firms choose rigid prices? Furthermore, in so far as the costs of adjustment are once and for all and the change in nominal demand is permanent, then a dynamic perspective is bound to alter the conclusion. In a dynamic perspective the losses from non-adjustment, however small for a single period, cumulate over time and are bound to weight the scales in favour of adjustment.

These are important observations. Nevertheless, it would be possible to meet these objections by allowing for quantity adjustment costs which are less than those of price adjustment and by allowing for problems in distinguishing permanent from transitory changes in nominal demand. But, it would make the argument depend rather too heavily on the actual contingencies of relatively costly quantity adjustments and difficulties of recognition. Fortunately, there is a rather more robust line of argument. It has two elements.

The first part notices that a change in nominal demand when others are not expected to adjust is experienced as a real change in demand by firms. The firms can know that their change in demand comes from a change in nominal demand, but if nobody else adjusts to the change it is not experienced as a nominal shock. It is experienced as a real shock because revenues change and there are no corresponding changes in costs. Whereas a change in nominal demand when everyone else is expected to adjust is experienced as a nominal shock demand because it will affect both revenues and costs. This difference leads directly into the second part of the argument.

The incentives towards adjusting prices depend on whether the shock is experienced as a real or nominal one (or to put this in a way which connects with the earlier point, the incentives depend critically on whether others are expected to adjust when it is nominal shock). This dependence arises for two reasons. First, this distinction is crucial for the evaluation in a dynamic context of the relative costs of quantity and price adjustment. The point here is that the least costly form of adjustment is unlikely to turn on the pure once and for all costs of adjusting price or quantity. Rather, it will depend on which form of adjustment is perceived as the permanent form of adjustment and which is only a temporary measure. Suppose, for instance, the demand change is experienced as a nominal shock, then in full equilibrium prices will adjust equiproportionately and quantities will remain unchanged. Plausibly, firms will realize this when deciding how to adjust to a perceived nominal shock and conclude that any price adjustment now is an instalment on what is required in the long run, whereas any quantity adjustment now will involve unnecessary costs because it will have to be reversed in the long run. Contrast this with the experience of a real demand shock. In full long-run equilibrium, there need be no change in relative price in response to such a shock. Indeed, in a variety of models, for instance where there is constant returns to scale technology and the shock does not produce a change in relative factor prices (that is, where the long-run supply function is horizontal), a real shock will only cause a change in quantities. In this context, any price adjustment in the short run will appear as unnecessary from the position of the long run and a source of needless adjustment costs; whereas, any quantity adjustment in the short run is a down-payment on what are unavoidable long run changes in quantity. Hence the costs of price adjustment relative to quantity adjustments seem high when others are not expected to adjust their prices, while quantity adjustment costs appear high when others are expected to adjust.

The second reason is that the profit loss from non-adjustment of price also varies with the expectation of compliance. Informally this can be observed in Figure 6.1. For instance, when other agents adjust to the nominal shock the costs of the monopolist will fall, both because wages fall and because the output of some firms are used as inputs by this firm. As costs fall, the rectangle B grows and this increases the loss from non-adjustment ($=B-A$).

More formally, I can rearrange equation 6.14 to make the same point.

$$P_i = aP^b M^{1-b} \tag{6.17}$$

Equation 6.17 gives the desired profit maximizing price and so the derivative of this with respect P or M shows how the optimal price changes when P or M change. When α and β both exceed one, as I have assumed, it follows that b is greater than zero and so a change in the general level of prices has a positive effect on the desired profit maximizing price. In other words, when others, say, adjust to an increase in the money supply by raising their prices (to produce a general increase in price) the profit maximizing price for a firm is higher than when the other firms do not adjust. Now, recall from equation 6.7 that the loss from non-adjustment of price depends on the gap between the current and optimal price, and we have the formal result that the loss from non-adjustment rises when others adjust their prices. (Strictly speaking, this result need not always hold even when we wish to maintain the diminishing returns assumption behind $\beta > 1$ and the finite price equilibrium assumption which lies behind $\alpha > 1$, since there is no need in general to have a unitary elasticity of demand for money balances.)

So to summarize the argument, we have reason for believing that the perceived profit losses of price non-adjustment in response to a nominal shock rise with the number of other agents expected to adjust (that is, the gains from price adjustment rise as numbers adjusting rise) and that the perceived cost of adjusting prices falls with the number of agents expected to adjust. These ideas are captured in Figure 6.2, and the potential for multiple equilibria is

Figure 6.2   Gains and costs of price adjustment

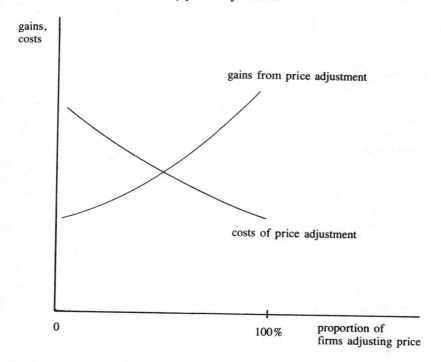

evident. As I have drawn it, there is one where nobody expects others to adjust: the demand shock is experienced as a real shock and consequently price adjustments appear relatively costly as compared with quantity adjustments and the gains from price adjustment appear relatively slight; the firms choose quantity adjustments. The other where everyone expects others to adjust, the demand shock is perceived as nominal and consequently the losses from non-adjustment of prices rise and costs of price adjustment seem relatively low compared with quantity adjustments; the firm chooses price adjustments. In this way, we have an explanation of why firms might choose not to adjust price which does not depend on *ad hoc* asymmetries between price and quantity adjustment and which does not ignore long-term considerations.

It leaves open, however, a rather important question. How does the economy select one set of self-fulfilling expectations rather than another? This is a coordination problem of the sort we have come across before, in Chapter 5 in connection with the selection of a rational expectations equilibrium, and it is discussed further in section 6.6.

To conclude this section, it is worth drawing out a particular aspect of the coordination problem which lurks here between wage and price setters, both because it does not depend on the specifics of the demand connections between firms and because it is a bridge to the discussion in the next chapter. Suppose, for instance, that firms are not expected to change their price in response to a decrease in the money supply; this encourages each individual not to change its price. Each firm perceives the shock as a real one and begins to adjust quantities. There is a reduction in the demand for labour and ordinarily one might expect that this will produce a fall in the real wage rate. To the extent that this does happen, inspection of 6.14 or 6.17 suggests that the profit maximizing price will fall by more than when the real wage does not change. With this greater fall, the costs from non-adjustment rise and there is additional encouragement to firms to change price. In other words, should the real wage not fall then this encouragement to price changes will not occur. Hence there is a connection between real wage stickiness and nominal price rigidity. Indeed the connection can be spun to bring out the coordination aspect between wage and price setting.

The story goes something like this. Imagine a fall in nominal demand. Price setters will want to adjust prices if they expect nominal wages will adjust. In the absence of this expectation, some real price stickiness (due say to menu costs) will prevent price adjustment. Wage setters are similarly placed. They want to adjust wages if they expect prices to adjust, but in the absence of such an expectation some real wage stickiness (for reasons yet to be discussed) prevents a wage adjustment. In such a setting, there will be (at least) two equilibria where expectations are confirmed by experience: one where neither firms nor workers expect each other to adjust and so both do not adjust; and one where both expect each other to adjust and so both do adjust. In this context, it is perhaps not surprising that some people have referred to situations where there is nominal wage and price rigidity as examples of coordination failures. Strictly speaking though, the failure is not with respect to coordination per se. Rather it is the coordination about the pareto inferior outcome which represents the failure.

6.5 Staggered Prices and Gradual Price Adjustment

This section explores how staggered price-setting contributes to price inertia. It is assumed that firms set prices at discrete points in time and hold them constant for an interval. This assumption has the virtue of realism because we rarely observe continuous price-setting, except in a few financial markets and primary commodities markets; and it can be understood as a simple response to the costs of price adjustment. Obviously, discrete pricing is a source of price inertia for the period of time that prices are fixed. Any change in the money supply which had not been anticipated at the time prices were set will not have an affect on the price level until firms set prices again. However, when price changes are also staggered across firms, the general level of prices exhibits a surprising degree of stickiness: the period of price adjustment extends well beyond the time it takes all firms to reset prices.

Informally, one can appreciate how this arises by drawing on the argument of the previous section. We know that the desired price change of any individual firm in response to a monetary shock is smaller when other firms do not adjust; and this form of partial individual price adjustment is built in by staggered price-setting. To illustrate the point, suppose some firms set their prices each month for a period of one year, that prices are at their full equilibrium values in December, and that there is an unanticipated increase in the money supply of x per cent on January. Only those firms setting prices in January will be able to adjust instantaneously; and since all others cannot adjust these firms will only adjust their prices some fraction of the x per cent which would be optimal if all were to adjust. In February, another group of firms get the opportunity to adjust. The general price will have increased slightly as a result of the actions of those setting prices in January, and so they will raise their prices by slightly more than those who set prices in January. Again, the adjustment will not be the full x per cent because this is only the optimal adjustment for the individual firm when the general price level has increased by x per cent. So we move on to March and some more firms raise price, by more than the February lot, but less than the x per cent, and so on. The adjustment proceeds until the last group of firms adjust their price in December. They too raise their prices, but by less than x per cent.

Consequently, one year after the shock, and even though each firm has had the opportunity to adjust to the shock, the price level has not adjusted by the full x per cent which is required to leave all real variables unchanged. Indeed, the same will still be the case one year later because, although the January (and later) setters have a further incentive to raise their prices because the general level of prices has risen since they first adjusted, they still will not want to raise price by the full x per cent, and so on. Hence, the adjustment of the general price level gets spread over a number of years even though each individual price is only fixed for one year. It is a direct consequence of the earlier argument about coordination and the inability to achieve perfect coordination when prices are staggered in this manner.

This argument can be presented more formally. I shall do it in a rather simpler setting where there are two firms, 1 and 2, each producing a commodity along the lines described in the previous section. Thus 6.17 gives the optimal price for each firm given the price of the other and the real supply of money. I shall approximate the general price level as a simple average of the log of the two individual prices, and by taking logs throughout, 6.17 becomes

$$p_1 = d + cp_2 + (1-c)m \qquad (6.18)$$

where $d=2a/(2-b)$ and $c=b/(2-b)$.

I now introduce some staggering. One firm sets prices in January (odd time periods, $t+1$, $t+3$ and so on) for one year (two time periods) and the other sets prices in June (even periods, t, $t+2$, and so on) for one year. Recalling the definition of p^* as the profit maximizing price, 6.18 can be rewritten in these circumstances as

$$p^*_t = d + cp_{t-1} + (1-c)m_t \qquad (6.19)$$

The firm setting price at t must take account of the fact that this price will hold for two time periods, and during the second period the other firm will have the opportunity to change its price. So setting price equal to the p^* given by 6.19 may not be optimal for the combined profits from both periods. To explore the choice of optimal price in this context, recall that the loss in each period depends approximately on the square of the difference between the actual price and its profit maximizing level (as in 6.7). I shall assume that profits in future periods are not discounted, so profit maximization over both periods becomes approximately the equivalent of minimizing

$$E(\text{loss}) = E[(p_t-p^*_t)^2 + (p_t-p^*_{t+1})^2] \qquad (6.20)$$

The solution to this problem yields the pricing rule,

$$p_t = 1/2(p^{e*}_t + p^{e*}_{t+1}) \qquad (6.21)$$

Substitution of 6.19 into 6.21 generates

$$p_t = d + (c/2)(p_{t-1} + p_{t+1}) + (m^e_t + m^e_{t+1})(1-c)/2 \qquad (6.22)$$

Since firm 1 is in a completely symmetric position to firm 2, the same equation can be derived for firm 2's optimal pricing. As a result, it is legitimate to solve this as a single difference equation in p even though different firms are setting prices in alternate periods. The stable solution can be derived by factorization. Ignoring the constant d, it is given by

$$p_t = \lambda p_{t-1} + [(1-c)/c]\lambda\Sigma_{i=0}[\lambda^i(m^e_{t+i} + m^e_{t+1+i})] \qquad (6.23)$$

where $\lambda = [1-\sqrt{(1-c^2)}]/c$ and lies between 0 and 1 for stability. To explore the implications of this price equation, I shall assume that the money supply follows a random walk with

$$m_t = m_{t-1} + u_t$$

So, the expected value of all future money supplies is given by the previous experienced level and 6.23 simplifies to

$$p_t = \lambda p_{t-1} + (1-\lambda)m_{t-1} \qquad (6.24)$$

Accordingly, $p_i = m$ in full equilibrium, but individual firm prices only adjust to this equilibrium after a change in the money supply gradually; and since the aggregate price level is an average of the individual prices, there is a similar inertia in the aggregate price level. To be specific, let me define the aggregate price level in this instance as p_t, then

$$p_t = 1/2(p_t + p_{t-1})$$

and substituting 6.24 yields

$$p_t = \lambda p_{t-1} + (1/2)(1-\lambda)(m_{t-1} + m_{t-2}) \qquad (6.25)$$

The intuition behind this result and the mathematics in this simple case are quite straightforward. An adjustment to a shock is spread over a number of periods because neither firm wishes to make the full adjustment when the other's price is fixed because this will put the firm at a relative competitive disadvantage. However, it does beg the question of why firms stagger prices.

One explanation of this pattern turns on the informational difficulties which a firm faces when trying to distinguish a real from a nominal shock in demand. Firms often just experience a change in demand and because the appropriate adjustment depends on whether it is a nominal or a real shock, the firm faces a problem of deciding whether it is a nominal or a real shock (see, for instance, the discussion in section 2.6). In this context, price changes by other firms provide useful information for a particular firm concerning nature of the demand shock and so each firm would like to set prices after all the others. However this is not possible for all firms and, instead, staggering can emerge as a solution to this information game between firms.

Before this explanation is developed in more detail, it may be helpful to make clear how this information problem differs from the one in the previous section. In the previous section, firms had no difficulty discerning an aggregate nominal shock. They knew when aggregate nominal demand had changed. Their information difficulty arose because a nominal shock could be experienced either as a nominal shock or a real shock depending on the reaction of other firms and individuals in the economy. The information problem could then be 'solved' by coordinating your behaviour/expectations with those of others: under one solution to this coordination problem prices adjusted, and under another solution prices did not adjust. In this section, the information problem precedes this coordination one. It concerns the perception of whether there has been a nominal change in aggregate demand.

I shall capture this information problem formally by introducing the assumption into this section's model that there is a two-period lag in the announcement of changes in the money supply and that there are random unobservable real shocks (e_j) that also affect each firm's demand function in any time period. Taking logs and ignoring inessential constants, this means that 6.13, the firm demand, becomes

$$y_j = (m-p) - \alpha(p_j-p) + e_j \qquad (6.26)$$

where $E(e_j)=0$, $E(e_j\ e_k)=0$ and $E(e_{jt}\ e_{jt+1})=0$. So the firm may experience a change in demand in a particular time period, but it cannot distinguish whether it is a real or a monetary shock. This may seem rather unrealistic as monetary statistics are frequently published and it may cast some doubt over this information extraction problem. However, it must be remembered that although the money supply gives all the information that is required for forming an expectation of nominal demand in this model, in general, it is not a sufficient statistic because there can be variations in the velocity of circulation. Accordingly, there is a general problem which firms face in knowing what is the state of aggregate nominal demand; and it is merely a convenient simplification to create this uncertainty in this model via a lack of information on the money supply. Again, I shall assume that the money supply follows a random walk. So, we know from the discussion of both staggered (that is, equation 6.24) and synchronized price-setting (that is equation 6.17) that when the firm sets price it will want to form an expectation of future money supplies and this expectation depends on the best estimate of the previous money supply.

Now, let us contrast the position of a firm under synchronization with the position of a firm under staggered prices. Take the synchronized case first for firms setting prices at t. All firms have knowledge of m_{t-3} and each firm will know the prices set at $t-3$. Furthermore, each firm will know from its own demand function (equation 6.26) what were the combined monetary and real shock realizations for itself for time periods $t-1$ and $t-2$ (that is, $m_{t-1} + e_{jt-1}$ and $m_{t-2} + e_{jt-2}$). But, it will not know what were the quantity sales of other firms, so it cannot infer from this knowledge, together with the fact that the sum of the real shocks equals zero, how to decompose the combined demand shock $(m+e)$ into its component nominal and real parts. That is, it will not be able to distinguish directly u_{t-1} and u_{t-2} (which affect m_{t-1} and m_{t-2} through the random walk hypothesis) from e_{jt-1} and e_{jt-2}, so it is forced to form a best estimate of u_{t-1} and u_{t-2} so as to obtain an estimate of future money supply levels on the basis of the information on the combined $u+e$ for each period.

In contrast, the position for a firm setting price at t when some other firms set price at $t-1$ is rather different. As before, the firm knows m_{t-3} and wishes to obtain an estimate of m_{t-1} to use when forming an expectation of current and future money supply levels. Again, as before, the firm will know from its own demand function the realizations of $u+e$ for $t-1$ and $t-2$. However, the firm also knows something else. It knows what were the prices set by the other group of firms in $t-1$. Further, it knows the choice of price for each firm setting price in $t-1$ depended on the shocks in $t-2$ and $t-3$ and on the price charged by the firms which set their price in $t-2$. Provided we assume that the sub-group of firms setting price at $t-1$ is sufficiently large, then we know that the real shocks in $t-2$ and $t-3$ sum to zero for this sub-group of firms, and so the average price set by this group of firms depends only on the money supply in $t-2$ and $t-3$ and on the price set by the other firms in $t-2$. The firms setting price at t know the money supply at $t-3$ and their own previous prices which they set at $t-2$, and so the information on the average price set at $t-1$ reveals information on the money supply at $t-2$. Thus, the firm setting price under the staggered arrangement has an easier task than its counterpart under synchronization. It knows m_{t-2} and only has to decompose the experienced shock in $t-1$ into its component parts in order to estimate m_{t-1} and thereby form an expectation of current and future money supply levels.

The demonstration that there is a gain from staggering does not prove that a staggered arrangement will emerge. The problem here is that, given the gains that come from coordinating your price with that of other firms, one might expect there would be a tendency to undermine any staggered arrangement. To appreciate the point in our model, suppose we started with two groups of firms setting prices in alternate periods and each group was of a similar size. From the point of view of coordinating your price with that of others, there is no gain to an individual firm from switching groups. However, imagine that there is a small switch of firms between groups so that the coordination gains from joining the larger group cease to be zero, then firms in the smaller group will want to switch to the larger group and in this way the staggered arrangement unravels as more firms wish to join the larger group.

This is undoubtedly a consideration, but it is unlikely to be decisive. Although the coordination gains provide an incentive to join the larger group, there is also likely to be a counterbalancing incentive to join the smaller group on information extraction grounds. The smaller group has a larger sample of prices (set by the larger group) from the previous period from which to infer the money supply of the period before that, as compared with the larger group (which only has the small group's prices as a sample). Thus, the greater efficiency in information extraction from larger rather than smaller sample sizes points to a counterveiling reason for joining small groups and stabilizing the staggered arrangement. So, to conclude this section, there is an information argument which explains why prices might be staggered and such staggering can impart stickiness to the aggregate price level.

6.6 'Trust' and the Costs of Price Adjustment: The Broader Role of Conventions in Price Determination

Until now we have accepted that there are costs of price adjustment. The existence of such costs may be self-evident in the sense that new price lists, catalogues, etc., need to be produced when prices are changed. Furthermore, it is typically costly to acquire the information about the state of demand, cost conditions, etc., which will enable a firm to calculate the optimal price. There is, however, another and perhaps less immediately obvious dimension to the costs of price adjustment. 'Inappropriate' price changes may undermine the 'trust' upon which certain mutually beneficial economic relationships are founded. This section provides a couple of illustrations of such costs of price adjustment.

In most microeconomic models, we tend to assume that information regarding the price and qualities of commodities comes free to purchasers. This is a useful simplification which allows us to go straight from a utility maximization problem, like that in section 6.4 to the derivation of market demands and the eventual solution of equilibrium prices. Nevertheless, it is unrealistic for many commodities and slides over 'search' – the activity of acquiring information.

Informally, it is easy to see why the introduction of search costs may be important for our understanding of the costs of price adjustment. When information is costly, what prevents all firms from trading on this ignorance by raising prices is individuals who acquire information and threaten to take their custom elsewhere. From a social perspective the acquisition of the information is a deadweight loss because the same full information price could be charged and the same trades could be undertaken by firms without the acquisition of information. If only firms could be 'trusted' not to raise price by trading on the ignorance of consumers, this deadweight loss could be avoided and both consumers and producers could be made potentially better-off.

In one-off interactions it is difficult for a firm to generate a reputation for 'trust' even though such a reputation might enable the pareto improvement that comes from the reduction in search. But in repeated interaction between a firm and the same consumers, in what are sometimes referred to as 'customer markets', firms have the opportunity of developing a reputation for 'trust' by demonstrating that they have not raised prices in the past (for a formal discussion, see section 4.4 where an analogous problem is examined). Since there is the gain that comes from reduced search, which can be distributed between consumers and firms through the choice of the price, it seems likely that firms will develop a reputation for trust when the opportunity arises in these customer markets.

However, the point about 'trust' is that it has to be nurtured through the actions of the firm and this requires careful attention to the circumstances in which a firm changes price and by how much. The circumstances must be such that both consumers and producers can observe that under the terms of the implicit agreement over price setting, a change in price is warranted. In other words, price adjustment does not just depend on firms acquiring the information on what is the necessary price adjustment. Consumers must also acquire the same information. In effect, the price is a negotiated price and both parties will agree to the price change only when both have acquired the same information and this may cause a delay in price adjustments. To do otherwise, to change price unilaterally when only the firm knows that such adjustment is appropriate is to incur a new sort of cost here because it threatens to undermine the 'trust' which has developed in economic relationships and which enables superior economic outcomes.

The point is actually more general than this example because 'trust' is also likely to arise in many settings between firms themselves. In this chapter, we have considered variants of the classic model of monopolistic competition, however in many market situations the interaction between firms corresponds more closely to a game which has prisoners' dilemma features. Take a standard example from duopoly theory where each firm has a choice between a 'high' and a 'low' price. Each firm does better when both price 'high' than when both price 'low' (the joint monopoly outcome as compared to the competitive outcome, if you like), but the best outcome for a firm is when it prices 'low' and the other firm prices 'high' because the 'low' price firm gobbles up market share. The worst outcome is conversely when a firm prices 'high' and the other firm prices 'low'. Figure 6.3 captures this preference ordering over the possible interactions between duopolists with some arbitrary pay-offs.

Figure 6.3 Duopoly game
$b > c > 0 > d$

firm 1 price

		high	low
firm 2 price	high	c, c	d, b
	low	b, d	$0, 0$

The game is similar to the one between the government and the private sector in section 4.4, in the sense that the Nash equilibrium in a one-shot version of the game (['low', 'low']) is pareto-dominated by another possible strategy pair (['high', 'high']). As before it is tempting to think that things would be rather different, in the sense that the pareto superior ['high', 'high'] outcome might emerge as an equilibrium, if the game were to be repeated. And indeed this is so. Either when the game is repeated indefinitely or when it is repeated finitely with some doubt in the minds of the firms about the motives of the other, the pareto superior outcome can be a perfect (or sequential) equilibrium. The intuition is the same as before. For instance, when the game is indefinitely repeated, the use of conditional punishment strategies means that it can become rational for each player to forego the short-run gain which comes from playing 'low' when the other plays 'high' because he or she thereby reaps the long-run gains which come from playing ['high', 'high'] in the future. I will demonstrate this in a moment for one particular punishment strategy, 'tit for tat' – section 4.4 can be consulted for a 'trigger' strategy in the same vein and for the case of finite repetitions. For now, the important point to notice is that the Folk theorem applies to these repeated games and this has implications for the discussion of price stickiness.

The Folk theorem tells us that these repeated games can have multiple perfect (or sequential) equilibria – and it is not difficult to see why since any variety of conditional strategies become possible and they can typically support any of a range of 'high' prices and a range of divisions of the spoils which come from implicit collusion. This poses a by now familiar selection problem. Explicit discussion and agreements on which equilibrium to choose are, of course, typically precluded by law and so the joint selection of the same equilibrium will have to come through firms conditioning their price setting on some shared piece of extraneous information. This is where conventions surface. They are an embodiment of these shared sources of extraneous information.

This pointer to conventions needs careful handling. Conventions select the equilibrium, but one might legitimately doubt whether this will prove a very significant contribution since on evolutionary grounds the monopoly price and an equal division of the spoils is likely to emerge, whatever happen to be the supporting strategies. However, shared conventions do something else when there is imperfect information. As in the earlier example of 'trust' in customer relations, they become a way of policing an implicit collusive agreement. To illustrate this aspect of their contribution, let us suppose that both firms wish to set a high price under their current strategies, but they operate with different information so that their estimates of the 'high' price differ at any moment in time. If each prices according to their estimate of what is the 'high' price to set, one will be setting a lower price relative to the other and will thereby threaten the implicit collusive arrangement. Firms will want to guard against these genuine misunderstandings either by having agreed conventions over how to interpret whether a 'low' price is a breach of the agreement or through following an agreed procedure (that is, convention) for calculating what is the high price in the first place. Now, the point about this aspect of the use of conventions is that the convention must turn on publicly-available information to avoid the problem of moral hazard associated with private information. In turn, this dependence can be a source of price inertia for the simple reason that many pieces of information on the state of demand start off in the private domain and can only gradually become public knowledge. Or to put the point slightly differently, to change price when it may first become obvious on the basis of private information alone will incur a cost in the form of undermining the trust that sustains a mutually beneficial economic relationship.

As promised, I shall conclude this section with a formal demonstration of the possibility of a 'tit for tat' equilibrium in the repeated version of this game. It is interesting because it offers one final insight on the sources of price stickiness. For this purpose, I assume that there is a probability π that in any play of the game it will be repeated. The 'tit for tat' (T) strategy involves playing 'high' first and then following whatever the other player has done in the previous round of the game. (It is like a one-period punishment strategy for cheaters as contrasted with the more draconian trigger strategy considered in Chapter 4, so it is perhaps more realistic. It has also typically performed well in tournaments.)

To show that T can be a best reply to itself, and hence that it is a perfect equilibrium, I shall exploit the nested structure of the decision problem when you play against someone using T. You know whether a T player will either play (a) 'high', or (b) 'low' because it depends on what you played in the last round. Suppose (a) first and I shall consider case (b) as part of this case below. Either (i) play 'high', or (ii) play 'low' is part of the best response. Consider (i) first. If play 'high' is part of the strategy that is a best response to this, then since you have played 'high' this round your opponent will play 'high' next round and the choice problem will repeat itself. Hence, if it was a best response to play 'high', it will be again, and so on. In other words, in these circumstances a strategy involving playing 'high' always would be a best response.

Now suppose (ii) holds. In this case your opponent plays 'low' in the next round. There are now two possibilities in this next round: either 'low' or 'high' are part of your best strategy response. (Notice, since the choice of initial round is arbitrary here, the following discussion also covers the case (b) above.) If 'low' is part of the best strategy response to 'low' then this will lead your opponent to play 'low' in the next round and the choice problem resurfaces in an identical manner, with the result that you play 'low', and so on thereafter. So, if your opponent is going to play low, and play low is part of the best response then you will play low thereafter. In other words, in these circumstances a strategy of 'low' always (L) would be a best response and a strategy T is not a best response to T.

Alternatively, suppose play 'high' is the best response to 'low'. Your opponent plays 'high' next round, and the decision problem returns to (a) above. We have ended up at (a) again by considering a possible best strategy which involves 'low' in the previous round, hence we have strategy which involves alternate 'high' and 'low' (A).

This exhausts all the possible responses to a T player and we find three candidate best responses: either play a strategy which involves 'high' (an example of which is T when the opponent is a T player) or play an L strategy or play an A strategy. It is now a matter of arithmetic to calculate the expected returns from each strategy so as to determine which is the actual best response in the circumstances.

$$E(T, T) = c(1+\pi+\pi^2+\ldots) = c/(1-\pi)$$

$$E(L, T) = b$$

$$E(A, T) = b+d\pi+b\pi^2+d\pi^3+b\pi^4+\ldots = (b+d\pi)/(1-\pi^2)$$

It can be seen from this that when $\pi > (b-c)/b$, $(b-c)/(c-d)$, the best strategy is T. Hence, provided the probability of repeat is sufficient, high [T, T] with ['high', 'high'] being played in each round is a perfect equilibrium for the game.

Let us pursue this briefly to bring out the implications for price stickiness. This condition is less likely to be satisfied when b increases. This is interesting because it means 'high' prices are less likely to obtain when the gains from cheating rise. This sounds intuitively plausible, and, when allied with the thought that it is during booms that the greatest gains from cheating are to be had (since the gain from grabbing market share expands with the size of the market), it adds to our understanding of price stickiness. To flesh this out, suppose an increase in nominal demand is experienced as a real shock by some duopoly market because firms and agents in other industries and markets have been slow to adjust price for whatever reason. The duopolists may wish to adjust prices upwards to take account of the nominal shock, but this adjustment could be muted by a switch to ['low', 'low'] from the collusive ['high', 'high'] equilibrium which occurs because the gains from 'cheating' rise during what is experienced by the duopolists as boom. So the normal price rise in response to an expansionary nominal shock is offset in some degree by a collapse of the implicit collusive arrangement and a price war.

6.7 Conclusion

Information and coordination have been at the heart of the discussion of price stickiness here. Three aspects of the information problem have had a direct bearing on the likely occurrence of sticky prices. First, there is a problem of not knowing what other agents in the economy are going to do in response to a nominal shock. This is important because your best price response often depends on coordinating what you do with others (as in section 6.3). Conventions with respect to price setting can act, quite rationally, as coordinating devices in these circumstances and the convention which is used need not produce quick price adjustments to nominal shocks.

Second, there is a problem of not knowing whether other agents in the economy are abiding by implicit agreements. 'Trust' is central to many economic transactions and it is only nurtured when untrustworthy behaviour can be easily detected and distinguished from the trustworthy variety. Again this involves the use of shared standards for behaviour (that is, conventions) which are conditional on publicly-available information. This dependence of pricing on public rather than private information in situations where 'trust' is at stake can also contribute to sluggish price adjustments.

Finally, there is an information difficulty with respect to distinguishing nominal from real shocks. Part of the problem relates here to anticipating the actions of others when the type of shock is known, but part of the problem relates to simply not knowing what type of shock has occurred. In these circumstances, an arrangement of staggered price-setting can plausibly arise because it is an information-generating device. However, the interdependence between optimal pricing in these circumstances can produce an extended period of price adjustments following a nominal shock.

Indeed, in one way or another it is the intertwining of information and interdependence which are the hallmark of this chapter. The world of perfect competition is very different to a world with poor information where there is a heightened awareness of interdependence. In one, prices adjust to clear markets quickly, and in the other, prices are naturally influenced by conventions and may only adjust sluggishly to nominal shocks.

6.8 A Brief Guide to the Literature

The introduction of price stickiness into an NCM model comes from Buiter (1980). The explanation of price stickiness through small menu costs and second order private losses is crystallized in Akerlof and Yellen (1985), and the existence of externalities asociated with price changes is neatly demonstrated in Mankiw (1985). Rotemberg (1982) and Blanchard and Kiyotaki (1987) are two of the early elaborations of the canonical NKM model of monopolistic competition. The recent formal discussion of the properties of economies with staggered pricing began with Taylor (1979 and 1980) on staggered wage setting and was extended to final price setting by Blanchard (1983). Cooper and John (1988) make the coordination aspects of equilibrium selection nice and explicit. The formal model where staggered pricing emerges as an equilibrium in an information game comes from Ball and Cecchetti (1988).

The ideas here, as in other parts of the discussion of price and wage stickiness, naturally predate these formal discussions: the most significant earlier contribution is to be found in the work of Okun (1975, 1981). He built on some earlier powerful insights from Alchian (1970) and emphasized the role of 'trust'. Tirole (1989) is an excellent source for game theoretic discussions of industrial pricing; the particular demonstration of 'tit for tat' follows Sugden (1986), and the connection with price stickiness during 'booms' is made by Rotemberg and Saloner (1986).

The relationship between these early ideas on price stickiness and the non-market clearing tradition of trading at false prices is rarely recognized by the New Keynesians, but it received its most comprehensive blending in a manner which emphasizes the information problems which arise from coordination difficulties in Leijonhufvud (1968). Gordon (1990) provides a useful survey of the field which reminds the reader of these connections.

Finally, the subject of conventions in price setting is relatively neglected in some senses, although there is plenty of applied work which finds evidence for a simple normal cost pricing rule of thumb. I leave it to the reader to consider how well such a convention might function to coordinate prices and how, more generally, the financial press, trade associations, accountancy practices and the like might also contribute to coordination and thereby equilibrium selection.

7. The New Keynesian Macroeconomics III: Wage Determination

7.1 Introduction

This chapter completes the discussion of the alternative New Keynesian microfoundations for macroeconomics by considering several non-market clearing accounts of real wage determination. At the risk of sounding excessively repetitive, let me remind you of why these accounts are important for macroeconomics.

First, they provide an explanation of why there might be some significant degree of real wage stickiness and this feeds directly into the demand management debate. (Such stickiness, of course, contrasts with the competitive model where a shift in demand would only *not* produce significant changes in the wage when the elasticity of labour supply is implausibly high.) One aspect of this connection is the way, it will be recalled from the last chapter, that such real wage stickiness strengthens the small menu cost explanation of price stickiness. Another aspect is that real wage stickiness can contribute to nominal wage stickiness. To see this possibility one need only replay here the argument relating real price stickiness to nominal price stickiness from Chapter 6. That is to say, if workers do not expect firms to adjust to the nominal demand shock then the shock is experienced as a real one and so any real wage stickiness will discourage wage adjustment in response to the nominal shock.

The similarity between these explanations of nominal stickiness in goods and labour markets makes it tempting to combine them. And indeed the temptation yields a coherent account of nominal wage and price stickiness which turns on a particular set of self-confirming expectations. Workers and firms might both want to adjust to a nominal shock if they expect each other to adjust. But when they do not expect each other to adjust, the incentive to adjustment is weaker, the shock is experienced as a real one and some small real wage and price stickiness can then forestall any price and wage adjustment. And of course, to remind you of the final leg in the argument, when nominal prices and wages are sticky, there is potentially a positive role for active demand management to influence employment.

Second, when real wages are not determined competitively so as to clear markets, the normative properties of NAIRU cease to be those of full employment (see Chapter 3) and we are encouraged to think of forms of supply-side activism. Under imperfect competition, the level of unemployment associated with anticipated inflation and complete nominal price and wage adjustment could be both undesirable and unstable as it becomes sensitive to supply-side shocks. In these circumstances, the key to supply-side policies directed at improving NAIRU lies with our understanding wage determination when perfect competition does not apply. Thus the discussion of the determination of wages is potentially relevant both to the conduct of aggregate demand management aimed at stabilizing output around the NAIRU value and to the use of supply-side policies directed at improving the NAIRU value itself.

The next section begins by considering some of the factors which make the labour market rather special and which render the competitive market model of wage determination of dubious relevance. Instead, wages are often set either explicitly or implicitly through some bargaining process. The following three sections present three related models of wage bargaining. It is not immediately obvious how best to characterize the explicit bargaining which takes place in labour markets and these three models offer different perspectives on the problem. Since each affords reasons for suspecting that real wages may be sticky, it is not important for us to decide between the models.

Section 7.6 introduces the 'efficiency wage' literature. This literature provides a final perspective on the imperfectly competitive determination of wages. It typically builds on the same special factors which I use to motivate the bargaining models, but it develops alternative models of wage determination to the competitive one without recourse to explicit bargaining theory. In this sense, these models can be regarded as complements to the bargaining models of sections 7.3, 7.4 and 7.5: they apply to labour markets where there are similar imperfections but where there is no explicit bargaining.

7.2   Some Important Features of Labour Markets: 'Trust' and Bargaining

As in some product markets, the problem of 'trust' often surfaces in labour markets. Consider, for instance, the acquisition of *specific* human capital which makes a worker more productive. The acquisition involves some effort on the part of a worker and leads to higher productivity. I assume the increase in output more than covers the amount which the employer would have to pay the worker to compensate for the expenditure of effort. So, the acquisition of specific human capital together with the payment of a higher wage can represent an opportunity for improvement to both parties. However, this pareto improvement is unlikely to occur unless the parties to the exchange 'trust' each other.

The problem is that the employer may offer to pay a higher wage but, once the worker has acquired the specific skill, the employer has no incentive to pay the higher wage. The employer can continue to pay the old lower wage without fear of the worker leaving because the skill has no value outside the firm and the worker's alternative employment opportunities have not changed (because the skill is firm specific). Furthermore, the employer has every incentive to do just this since he or she will thereby reap all the gains from the acquisition of the skill: all the increase in output is enjoyed as increased profits. So, unless the worker can 'trust' the employer not to renege in this manner, he or she will decide not to acquire the skill because it requires effort. Figure 7.1 makes the problem clear by presenting the decision in an explicit game theoretic context. In this figure I have assumed that the gain to output from acquiring the human capital is £150, that the effort required is the equivalent of £50, and that before the acquisition of human capital, net output per worker is £200 and this is divided equally between the worker and the employer.

Figure 7.1   Game of trust

		employer	
		'high' wage	'low' wage
worker	'high' effort	£150, £150	£50, £250
	'low' effort	£200, 0	£100, £100

In effect, the worker and the employer are involved in a prisoner's dilemma game and the Nash equilibrium of (low wage, low effort) is a pareto inferior outcome. It is not difficult to think of other aspects of the exchange between workers and employers which also embody prisoner's dilemmas. For instance, most wage contracts usually only specify that the worker should be on site for a number of hours, they do not specify the effort that the worker should expend. Yet, typically, most activities will give some discretion to the worker over the level of effort. To keep matters simple: he or she can work with high or low effort. The employer can pay a high or a low wage, and both parties might benefit from the [high wage, high effort] trade. Nevertheless, this trade of effort for a higher wage will not occur because the employer realizes that the worker has every incentive to expend a low effort once the high wage has been paid and this produces a worse outcome for the employer than settling for the [low wage, low effort] outcome. In this instance, the problem of 'trust' attaches to the workers' side of the bargain.

It is tempting to imagine that these prisoner's dilemmas can be unlocked through the introduction of an explicit contract that makes, for example, the high wage conditional on high effort. However, writing such contracts is not always easy. First, it is difficult to cover every contingency, simply because the world is too uncertain, yet to renegotiate every time there is a change in the environment would be extremely costly. Second, the information on performance is often impacted, creating problems of moral hazard in some instances in the execution of a contract. Or, even when both parties know about performance, this information is not available to third parties who might be called upon to adjudicate and give force to the agreement when disputes arise between the contracting parties.

The labour market illustrates these contracting problems well. Whether the worker has expended high effort or not is really only known with certainty by the worker. The employer may suspect from his or her pay-offs that the worker has not expended effort. But, in the absence of a fully contingent contract, the worker could always claim that the employer's profits are low because of other developments which were unforeseen and which are completely unrelated to effort. And even when the employer and the worker each know that there has not been performance, to enforce the contract they have to be able to demonstrate this to the courts and this requires publicly-available information on performance.

Nevertheless, these problems might be overcome. A contract can be made enforceable without the need to appeal to some adjudicating and enforcement agency like the courts. When a game of this sort is repeated it is possible for each party to provide the means of enforcement by threatening not to cooperate in the future if there is not compliance in the present (as in 'tit for tat' strategies). We have already seen how this becomes possible in the discussion of a similar repeated game in Chapter 6. Since most interactions between employers and workers will be repeated, it seems likely that 'trust' will be generated in the relationship through strategies involving threats (particularly if the company is to survive in a competitive environment). There are, however, two points that follow from our earlier discussion of 'trust' which it is useful to bring out for the general argument of this chapter.

First, in so far as the problem of 'trust' is overcome in a repeated setting with the employment of 'tit for tat' or other conditional/punishment strategies, then the precise pair of strategies will involve a solution to the issue of how the gains from 'trust' are to be distributed between the two parties. In the example above, the joint value of trust is £100 and I simply assumed in Figure 7.1 that this was equally divided between the two parties. However, in general, any distribution which pays either party something above £100 offers an incentive to both to generate 'trust' in the relationship; and so the issue of how the gains from 'trust' are to be distributed remains open. To put this rather more formally, the Folk theorem in game theory suggests that all repeated games have a number of perfect equilibria. So, there remains a question of how one equilibrium is selected. Since, these equilibria differ in part according to the distribution of the benefits between the players, it may be sensible to study equilibrium selection as a bargaining game. This suggests we will have to understand something about bargaining if we are to understand how the actual wage moves in an economy, because implicitly, at least, a particular solution to the 'trust' problem will involve elements of bargaining.

Second, whatever implicit or explicit agreement agents might like to make through bargaining in an ideal world (and I turn to this in later sections), the actual agreement will have to take account of the informational difficulties we have noted. This is likely to have some consequences for the question of wage stickiness which are similar to those discussed in the last chapter.

At the risk of repetition again, suppose agents would like to make a contingent agreement where one of the contingencies is the state of final commodity demand, then these informational difficulties are likely to contribute to wage inertia. We can see this because contingent agreements have to rely on publicly-available information or on private information which will be revealed truthfully. In the case of the former, the time which it takes for signals which are first experienced privately to become incorporated in public statistics is likely to impart some sluggishness to all adjustments, including wages. In the case of the latter, there are two possibilities worth mentioning. One encourages truthful revelation of private information because the private information can be checked later against public information. In which case truthful revelation will occur if it is part of a repeated game solution which produces 'trust' – truthful revelation is the same as not cheating in the game and can be supported by a suitable punishment strategy. To work, this does depend on private information seeping into the public domain in some unvarnished fashion and this may not always happen, particularly if the party claiming access to the private information can affect how it appears in the public domain. Alternatively, or as part of the above, a contract may be written which encourages truthful revelation of private information. Here, there is an interesting asymmetry between contingent agreements which specify wage adjustments in response to demand variations and those that specify employment adjustments. This can be appreciated with the aid of a simple example.

Suppose the firm's real revenue function is given by $R(L,B)$ where L is the level of employment and B is an index of the state of the cycle (it can be thought of as capturing cyclical movements in productivity or real product demand, or nominal stickiness elsewhere in the economy, etc., depending on your view of the cycle), and where R_L, R_B, R_{LB} are all >0. Figure 7.2 illustrates a cyclical movement in the marginal revenue product function. The real profits are given by $R(L,B)-(W/P)L$ and for a given wage they will be maximized

Figure 7.2   Relative incentives to dissemble

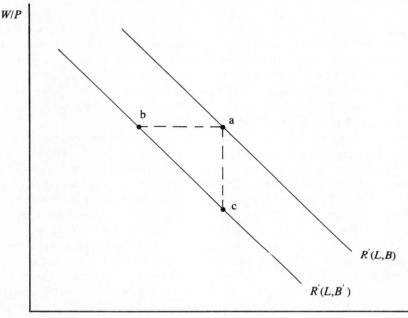

in the usual way by equating the marginal revenue product with the wage. I assume that the preferred wage-employment combination is given by point 'a' for the cyclical state *B*. Now, consider two polar possible contingent agreements: one which has variations in employment as in the movement to point 'b' when the cycle is at *B'*; and the other which only has variations in the wage as in the movement to point 'c'. Focus on the incentive that exists towards dissembling under the two agreements, that is, of claiming that the cycle is at *B'* when in fact it is at *B*. A movement from 'a' to 'b' when the cycle is actually at *B* will lower firm profits. While a movement from 'a' to 'c' will raise profits when the cycle is actually at *B* (this may be obvious but if it is not then return to this after the discussion around Figure 7.5).

In other words, pure quantity adjustment contingent agreements do not provide an incentive to dissemble while price adjustment agreements do. Hence, in so far as we do observe contingent agreements, they seem more likely to involve quantity adjustments rather than price adjustments. Quite simply, even when parties may want to have ones which specify significant wage responsiveness, the incentive which exists to dissemble under wage sensitive contracts means that these sort of contracts are less likely to be written or made.

To conclude this section, it is perhaps worth noting that there are other factors which reinforce the suggestion that implicitly or explicitly bargaining contributes to wage determination. For instance, the simple costs of hiring and firing will mean that the wage can take on any value between the worker's next best alternative and a premium above this which is given by those hiring and firing costs. In addition, of course, we know that there are institutions like trade unions which explicitly bargain with employers. Nor is it difficult to understand why those who suffer unemployment when there is bargaining do not attempt to bid down the wage. There is much evidence which points to the role of social conventions in labour markets which tell against this behaviour; and from the vantage point of the theory of clubs, it should come as no surprise that these conventions might exist.

Thus, to summarize, there are a variety of reasons for supposing that wage determination depends on bargaining. I have focused on how the existence of 'trust' creates a benefit which will be bargained over, both because I suspect that these benefits are ubiquitous in the labour market and because the difficulties associated with the generation and maintenance of 'trust' immediately point us in the direction of expecting some wage stickiness.

7.3 The Monopoly Union Model

There are many models of wage bargaining. The simplest model casts the union as a monopoly supplier of labour which sets the wage unilaterally. As such, it is not really a bargaining model even though it recognizes a key bargaining institution, trade unions. Nevertheless, it affords a useful starting point and there are probably some 'bargained' wages which correspond to this model. The analysis proceeds along the lines of the standard monopoly price-setter and it requires a specification of union objectives. I shall suppose that the union attempts to maximize the expected utility of its representative member; and utility is an additively separable function of the wage received and the disutility of work (D). Thus, the expected utility of the representative worker when there are N members of the union and L are employed is written as

$$E(U) = L/N[U(W/P) - D] + (1-L/N)[U(A)] \qquad (7.1)$$

where A is the alternative wage, that is the sum which the worker will enjoy when he or she is not employed at this unionized firm. In the case where the alternative is unemployment, it can be thought of as the unemployment benefit. More generally, it will also depend on wages elsewhere together with the probability of re-employment elsewhere.

There are a variety of ways in which this particular objective function might be justified (see Oswald, 1985). One has it as a 'utilitarian' objective function by noticing that, since N and D are given as far as the union is concerned, the maximization of this function amounts to the maximization of

$$L[U(W/P) - U(W/P^*)] \tag{7.2}$$

where W/P^* is defined as the reservation wage, that is the wage such that $U(W/P^*)=D+U(A)$. In other words, it is the equivalent of maximizing the utility gain from employment at this firm for the membership as a whole.

The union maximizes this function subject to the constraint of the firm's labour demand function. To develop this, I shall assume again that the firm's real revenue is a function of the level of output and hence employment (L) and the state of demand (B) $(=R(L,B)$ with R_B and $R_{LB} > 0$). Hence real profits are given by

$$R(L,B) - (W/P)L \tag{7.3}$$

And the profit maximizing demand for labour is given implicitly by the first order condition

$$R_L(L,B) = W/P \tag{7.4}$$

Thus the first order conditions for the union maximization of 7.2 subject to 7.4 yields

$$[U(W/P) - U(W/P^*)]/U'(W/P) = -LR_{LL}(L,B) \tag{7.5}$$

Dividing both sides by W/P $(=R_L(L,B))$, this becomes

$$[U(W/P) - U(W/P^*)]/(W/P)U'(W/P) = -[LR_{LL}(L,B)]/(W/P) \tag{7.6}$$

The left-hand side of this expression is the reciprocal of the elasticity of the utility gain from employment with respect to the wage, and the right-hand side is the reciprocal of the elasticity of labour demand with respect to the wage. Accordingly, when cyclical movements in demand leave these elasticities unchanged, the real wage which satisfies this first order condition will also be unchanged. In other words, the real wage becomes invariant to cyclical changes in demand.

This is actually the standard result from the monopoly pricing model which finds that a firm with a constant marginal cost will set a price which depends on the elasticity of demand. So price is constant whenever there is an isoelastic shift in demand. The only trick to notice in the transposition to the labour market of this standard result is that the equivalent of the constant marginal cost for the union is a constant disutility of work and alternative wage as this is what the union member gives up when he or she gains employment. However, it might be reasonable to suppose that the reservation wage actually changes with the level of aggregate employment, since, in general, the reservation wage will depend on alternative employment opportunities and these rise in a boom and fall in a recession even when the unemployment benefit does not vary over the cycle. In these circumstancs, we should expect some pro-cyclical movement in wages even when demand shifts isoelastically.

It is worth exploring the connection with the standard monopoly model in a little more detail both to help with the intuitions and because it reveals an interesting parallel with the earlier menu costs discussion of price stickiness. Let us suppose that individual utility from work is a linear function of the wage and the disutility of work, and we choose units so that utility of a wage is equal to its real value – this is the equivalent of assuming that workers are risk neutral because $U(\pounds x) = \pounds x$ in these circumstances. Then, 7.2 becomes

$$L[W/P - W/P^*]$$

This has exactly the same form as the conventional monopoly profit function: W/P^* the equivalent of per unit costs, W/P is the per unit revenue, and L

Figure 7.3 Non iso-elastic shifts in demand

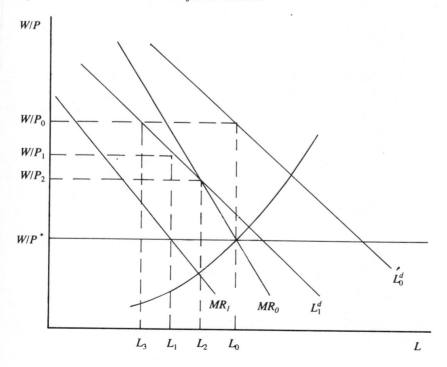

gives the quantity sold. Once the problem takes this conventional form, it can be seen that the earlier arguments with respect to small menu costs of price adjustment also apply here and may help explain stickiness in cases when demand does not shift isoelastically. A non-isoelastic shift is depicted in Figure 7.3, and utility maximization requires a change in the wage from W/P_0 to W/P_1. However, the adjustment may not occur because the gain from altering the real wage when there is a constant reservation wage is of second order significance. This is apparent in Figure 7.4 where the utility loss from non-adjustment is made explicit: it is equal to the difference in the area of the shaded rectangles B and A. If there are small menu costs associated with changing the wage then this second order gain may not be sufficient to warrant the change. Again, we can see from Figure 7.3 that the argument for stickiness is qualified when W/P^* moves pro-cyclically (the equivalent of an upward sloping marginal cost curve) because the desired change in the wage in response to the shift in demand is greater (from $W/P)_0$ to $(W/P)_2$). Remembering the earlier Taylor expansion of the loss associated with non-adjustment, it follows that the losses grow as the gap between the actual and optimal price increases.

Figure 7.4   Menu costs gain

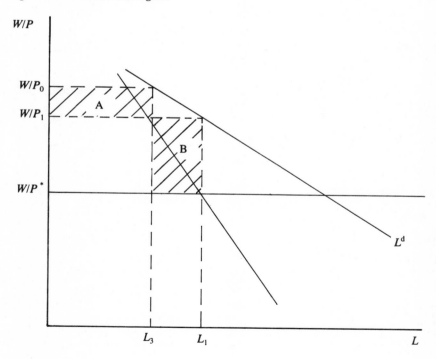

These connections are useful reminders of the small menu cost argument. (The use of the argument in Chapter 6 might beg the question of what are the menu costs in this new setting? But there is a plausible short answer in the form of negotiation costs analogous to the costs of changing catalogues, price lists, etc., coupled with costs of endangering 'trust' when it arises in labour market relationships.) This application of an argument from the previous chapter should, perhaps, come as no surprise because wage and price setting are similar activities. Indeed, it is not the only connection: the other major argument in Chapter 6 which turned on staggered price-setting also has an exact parallel in an argument with staggered wage-setting. It aids the understanding of wage stickiness to note the potential relevance of the earlier staggered setting argument but it serves no purpose to repeat the formal modelling of staggered pricing now – so, take it as read! Instead, I shall turn now to a new model, an explicit model of bargaining.

7.4 A Bargaining Model

The monopoly union model (along with other models which locate the wage employment decision on the labour demand curve) is often criticized because

Figure 7.5 Efficient bargains

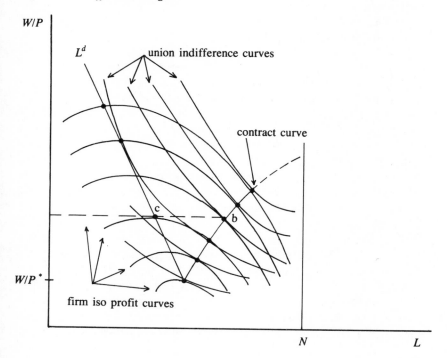

the bargains struck along the labour demand curve are inefficient. The criticism can be appreciated with the aid of Figure 7.5.

In this figure, I have plotted the isoprofit curves based on equation 7.3, assuming a given value for B. Lower isoprofit curves represent higher profit levels. For a given wage the firm maximizes profits by operating on the highest isoprofit curve, and this will be achieved when the slope of the isoprofit curve is zero at that wage rate. The locus of these points where the slope is zero gives the labour demand function. The union indifference curves are the graphical representation of equation 7.1 (or 7.2). At the wage W/P^*, the union gains nothing from supplying labour and so the slope of each indifference curve approaches zero at this wage.

Under the monopoly union model, the union takes the labour demand function as a constraint and seeks the wage level which achieves the highest indifference curve. Suppose this occurs at point 'a' in the Figure 7.5. However, this is obviously not efficient: there are other feasible wage and employment combinations, like 'b', which would make both the firm and the union better-off. The locus of efficient bargains, the contract curve in this context, is given by the points of tangency between the isoprofit and indifference curves. It will start at where W/P^* intersects with the labour demand (because we know that the slope of all indifference curves approach zero at this wage rate and the isoprofit function with a slope of zero at this wage gives us the labour demand at this wage) and it will move in a north-easterly direction.

It is perhaps worth noting that although the wage bargains on the labour demand are not efficient, except when they correspond to the competitive outcome with $W/P = W/P^*$, they are still sometimes defended as the most likely outcomes. One reason which has been advanced is that although efficient wage contracts commend themselves, we typically observe bargaining over wages and not employment. And when a wage is agreed to, the profit maximizing firm will choose an employment level on the labour demand function. So, for instance, the argument goes: the firm and the union might agree that 'b' is superior to 'a', but if this leads the union to agree to the wage at 'b', the profit maximizing firm will choose an employment level at 'c'. The combination at 'c' is worse for the union than 'a'. Thus, with bargaining over wages alone, the union would do well to treat the labour demand function as the feasible set.

This argument has some plausibility. However, as with many one-shot games, the results are rather different when the game is repeated. In these circumstances, there will typically be perfect equilibria with conditional/punishment strategies which produce efficient bargains, or sequential equilibria where the firm will want to fuel a reputation for not behaving opportunistically once an efficient wage bargain has been struck (see sections 4.4 and 6.6). So, the contract curve does seem a reasonable starting point in a repeated setting. (Even if you are not convinced by this, the following discussion applies equally to bargaining on the labour demand function.)

The immediate question now becomes how is the precise wage and employment pair determined and how will it be affected by changes in the cyclical state of demand (that is, by variations in B)?

Let me begin with the easier second part of that question. We know that the contract curve is given by points of tangency between indifference curves and isoprofit curves, and this condition is given by

$$- [U(W/P) - U(W/P^*)]/U'(W/P) = [R_L(L,B) - W/P] \qquad (7.7)$$

Partially differentiating this with respect to B, I obtain

$$\partial(W/P)/\partial B = [R_{LB}(L,B)U'(W/P)^2]/\{[U(W/P) - U(W/P^*)]U''(W/P)\}$$

and with a concave utility function, this will be negative. In other words a cyclical upswing producing a higher B means that for any given level of L, the wage on the contract curve is lower.

To complete the analysis of how the contract curve is affected by cyclical swings, we should take account of the possible influence via changes in the reservation wage. This is done by partially differentiating 7.7 with respect to W/P^*

$$\partial(W/P)/\partial(W/P^*) = - [U'(W/P)U'(W/P^*)]/\{[U(W/P) - U(W/P^*)]U''(W/P)\}$$

Through inspection, this is positive. So, any cyclical influence via the reservation wage tends to move the contract curve in the opposite direction to changes in the marginal revenue product function. In what follows, I shall assume that the changes in marginal revenue product dominate the effects of movement in the reservation wage.

This leaves me with the rather more awkward part of the question: What employment wage pair is chosen from a given contract curve? Nash provides the most celebrated solution to this problem. (NB: This bargaining solution is not to be confused with the Nash equilibrium concept which we have used in non-cooperative games.) His initial approach was axiomatic. He specified several axioms and discovered that every bargaining game has only one solution which satisfies them. To present these axioms, it helps to characterize bargaining games in terms of pay-offs and threat or conflict points. The pay-offs are the range of returns which become available upon agreement – our contract curve mapped into the pay-off space. The threat or conflict points are the returns to each player when there is no agreement – in our bargaining game, if we assume that a failure to agree results in no employment and no production by the firm, then the conflict points are NU(W/P^*) for the union and zero for the firm in the absence of fixed costs.

The first axiom establishes the rationality of both parties and has the effect of singling out pareto-efficient outcomes.

The second axiom demands that solutions should be invariant to linear transformations of either party's pay-offs. So, it should not matter to the solution whether the firm measures its pay-offs in pounds or pence.

The third axiom specifies 'independence of irrelevant alternatives'. In this context, this means that if [x] is a solution to a bargaining game, then [x] should be the solution to another bargaining game which has the same conflict points but a different pay-off space, provided this new space contains [x]. To illustrate what this implies, let us assume there is a game where £100 is to be divided between two players, A and B, and each gets zero when there is no agreement. Let us suppose the solution to this game is £50 each. Then, this axiom holds that £50 should also be the solution to another game where £100 is to be divided between the same two players subject to the proviso that player A should not get less than £40.

The final axiom requires symmetry when the game is completely symmetrical as far as each player is concerned. So, if it makes no difference to the description of the game from each player's perspective when A takes over B's role and vice versa, then the pay-offs to both players should be the same.

Nash shows that the unique solution that satisfies these axioms in all games is the outcome which maximizes the product of the gains from agreement which each party enjoys. In our game, this means the Nash solution is found by maximizing

$$[R(L,B) - (W/P)] \{ L[U(W/P) - U(W/P^*)] \} \qquad (7.8)$$

subject to the constraint of the contract curve.

The first order conditions which come from maximizing 7.8 turn out to imply that real wage is the average of the marginal and the average product of labour. That is,

$$W/P = [(1/L)R(L,B) + R_L(L,B)]/2 \qquad (7.9)$$

Under the assumptions we have made, 7.9 is a decreasing function of L and it will shift outward during a boom ($dB > 0$) and inward during a recession ($dB < 0$). In Figure 7.6, the contract curve and the general Nash condition from equation 7.9 have been drawn, and we find the unique Nash bargaining solution is given by the intersection of the two curves. I have also plotted the effects of a boom on both these curves to see how the Nash solution changes under

Figure 7.6   Nash bargains

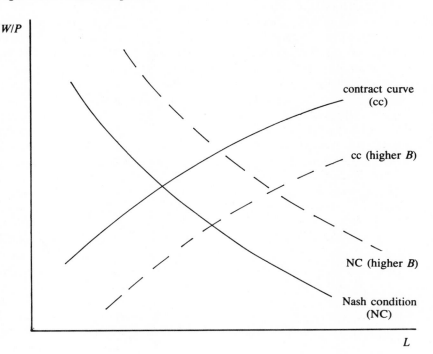

W/P

contract curve
(cc)

cc (higher *B*)

NC (higher *B*)

Nash condition
(NC)

L

boom conditions. Interestingly, both curves shift to the right producing a relatively small change, with ambiguous sign, in the real wage and a large increase in employment. In short, the Nash solution to a bargaining game predicts real wage stickiness under the assumptions we have made about how cyclical changes affect the game.

From our point of view, this is an important result which appears to complement the one developed in the previous section. However, there are two reasons for being cautious. First, both results depend on discounting in one way or another the effects of cyclical change on the reservation wage. In the monopoly union model, pro-cyclical movements in the reservation wage made real changes more likely. Likewise, here pro-cyclical movements will tend to mitigate the movements in the contract curve and increase the likelihood of pro-cyclical bargained real wage movements. There is nothing wrong with being cautious on this score. This is as it should be since we have a theoretical explanation of wage stickiness which holds contingently.

The second reason for being cautious is rather different and relates to the applicability of the Nash solution. This is not the place to discuss bargaining theory in any detail but several comments are worth making because they reinforce the general argument of this book.

Some people have taken Nash's axioms to have an obvious applicability because rational bargainers would recognize their applicability and hence incorporate them into the solutions which they groped towards. The question then becomes: Do the axioms really commend themselves to all rational players?

Plainly any answer to this question will depend on how rationality is defined. But, game theory (and most of economics) works with a straightforward instrumental conception of rationality (that is, agents act so as to satisfy best their preferences/objectives). Further, it is assumed that each agent knows that each agent is rational in this sense and so rational beliefs about others are those which are consistent with everyone recognizing that each is instrumentally rational. In short, beliefs about others should be confirmed by the instrumental behaviour of others. What is not clear is that this conception of rationality will make Nash's axioms self-evidently applicable to bargainers. For instance, why should this conception of rationality demand symmetry? Suppose there is £100 to be divided between two players who value pounds in exactly the same way (as in the example of the gain which comes from trust in the example around Figure 7.1), then the Nash solution with symmetry has each player getting £50. But, suppose each player believes that the taller person will claim £70 and the shorter person £30. Given this belief, the instrumentally rational taller person will claim £70 and the shorter person will claim £30 since the best claim that the taller person can make given this belief is £70 and likewise £30 is the best claim for the shorter person. Thus the belief is self-confirming and we have no reason for rejecting the (£70, £30) on grounds of instrumental rationality and the admissability of only those beliefs which are confirmed by experience. Of course, this solution requires that there should be a convention that tall people get 70 per cent, and one can imagine any number of possible conventions which might exist in societies and different conventions which would produce different outcomes. Indeed, one possible convention is that of symmetry. But, symmetry is just that: it is a convention on par with that of any other. We have to agree to ignore all other attributes like height if the symmetry convention is to work, just as we have to agree to be guided by height if the 'tall person gets 70 per cent' convention is to work. The claims of symmetry as far as instrumentally rational agents are concerned is no greater than the claim of any other convention which would allocate the £100.

Likewise, it is not clear why the independence of irrelevant alternatives axiom should appeal to instrumentally rational agents who hold beliefs which are confirmed by experience. This is a restriction on belief which helps to narrow down the candidates for how to divide the £100, but its status is no different from that of the restriction on belief which comes from the convention of appealing to height.

With the recognition of these sort of difficulties, many people have tried to justify the Nash solution in a different way. They have modelled particular plausible systems of bargaining and they have argued that the outcome of such bargaining procedures is the Nash solution (or something which approximates Nash).

There are two difficulties with this approach. First, Nash will only have been shown to be appropriate to those particular bargaining systems. Second, it is not clear that the solutions to these bargaining games do not rely on 'importing something' to produce the Nash solution that goes beyond what can be justified by the appeal to rationality. Two rather famous attempts along these lines, due to Zeuthen-Harsanyi and Rubenstein, seem to rely on such arbitrary 'importations'. For example, let us consider briefly the Zeuthen-Harsanyi tradition.

We assume the two players have conflict points c_1 and c_2 and that player 1 makes an offer to divide some cake of $[v_1, v_2]$ and that player 2 makes a counter offer of division of $[w_1, w_2]$; where $v_1 + v_2 = w_1 + w_2$, but $v_1 > w_1$ and $v_2 < w_2$ and so we have a conflict. The question is which party is going to concede and revise his or her offer? The answer supplied by this tradition comes from considering the level of fear each party has of a fight, called a risk limit. Suppose p_1 is the probability assessment 1 has that 2 will not concede, then the expected return to 1 of sticking to his or her last offer is $p_1 c + (1-p_1)v_1$ and the return from conceding is w_1. Consequently, player 1 will only stick to his or her last offer if

$$p_1 c_1 + (1-p_1)v_1 \geq w_1$$

that is, if

$$p_1 \leq (v_1 - w_1)/(v_1 - c_1) = r_1$$

where r_1 is defined as the highest probability of conflict that player 1 will face rather than concede (this is 1's risk limit). Likewise we can derive r_2 as

$$r_2 = (w_2 - v_2)/(w_2 - c_2)$$

Now it is argued that whichever party has the lowest risk limit will be the first to concede and when the two risk limits are identical both will concede. It follows that the player whose offer implied the lower Nash product of the gains from dividing the pie will be the one to concede, since when $r_1 \geq r_2$ then $(v_1 - c_1)(v_2 - c_2) \geq (w_1 - c_1)(w_2 - c_2)$. Accordingly, at each stage in the bargaining process the offer with the lowest Nash product of gains will be replaced by one which is higher and the process will end when the offer with maximum product of the gains has been reached. In other words, when the Nash solution to the bargaining game obtains.

The difficulty with this approach is that it relies on the assumption that the player with the lowest risk limit will concede first and it is not obvious why this should be the case if all we are allowed to assume is common knowledge of common instrumental rationality. Plainly, if both players accepted this convention then it would produce behaviour consistent with the convention and so it would be rational in the rational expectations sense (or the common knowledge of rationality sense of game theory), but there are any number of conventions which would also do this. For instance, suppose players believe that the player with lowest number should concede. Then player 1 expects 2 will stand firm and rationally decides to concede while 2 expects 1 to concede and rationally decides to stand firm. The convention produces beliefs which are confirmed by the subsequent behaviours and yet this need not produce concessions in line with the Zeuthen-Harsanyi convention since nothing has been said about the rs here and 1 conceding would be consistent with $r_1 > r_2$. In short, it seems that there must be something other than rationality that explains the use of the Zeuthen-Harsanyi convention and which is responsible for the Nash solution. (Likewise the Rubinstein (1982) approach depends on a presumption, which seems to have nothing to do with rationality, that eventually there would be a unique solution which emerged from his bargaining process.)

At root the problem is that bargaining seems bound to involve elements of a chicken game and there are always more than one equilibrium to such games. To appreciate this suppose we are back with the squabble over £100. The two sides come to the table and each issues a demand. The interesting case arises when the two demands exceed £100: let us say both players demand £60. In the next stage of bargaining, each must decide whether to accept the other's offer or refuse it. The pay-offs at this stage are given in Figure 7.7.

Figure 7.7   Chicken game

player B

		accept	refuse
	accept	£40, £40	£40, £60
player A	refuse	£60, £40	0, 0

There are two Nash equilibria in pure strategies and there is a mixed strategy equilibrium in this game. (NB: We have returned to Nash equilibrium concept for non-cooperative games here and this is not the Nash solution to the bargaining game!) We can exclude the latter because it is pareto inferior, but we are left with no way of predicting which of the two others will emerge. If there is a convention in the form of a shared belief concerning what to expect in these circumstances then we will know what outcome to expect. But, by definition, this convention will turn on extraneous information and in principle this could involve almost anything. However, in this particular instance, since we are discussing the division of a cake, we might suspect that the extraneous information will involve shared ideas concerning justice. This observation may not tell us exactly what to expect, but at least it points us in the direction of where to look for the sources of extraneous information.

One candidate convention along these lines has been studied in the literature: it associates a 'fair' division of net revenue between workers and employers with a constant share. Mathematically, in our earlier bargaining model between a union and a firm this amounts to

$$(W/P)L = kR(L,B) \qquad (7.10)$$

where 'k' is the 'fair' share.

In these circumstances, plotting 7.10 together with our contract curve will yield the solution to the bargaining problem. Equation 7.10 will be downward sloping in the $[W/P,L]$ space and it will move in the same direction in response to the cycle as the Nash solution, equation 7.9. Consequently, it generates the same predictions with respect to wage stickiness.

This brings us back to the same conclusion. Admittedly we have really only considered two conventions which might be used in the bargaining game. But the insights are useful nevertheless and suggest that we should not be surprised theoretically if we found real wage stickiness as a result of bargaining in the real world. Indeed, in so far as there is some real wage stickiness, it will come through the influence that pro-cyclical movements in the reservation wage have on the wage bargain (as in the monopoly union model). And whatever is the wage sensitivity from this source, we know that it can never be as great as we would expect under competitive arrangements. We know this because under competitive conditions the wage will move so as to clear the market (that is, no change in unemployment), whereas under these imperfectly competitive arrangements the wage is only likely to change in so far as the reservation wage changes and this will only change when there is some alteration in the level of unemployment. (The point here is that, in general, the reservation wage depends not only on unemployment benefits but also on the probability of re-employment if you lose this job. Thus a fall in the reservation wage will only occur, in the absence of a fall in unemployment benefits, when there is a rise in unemployment which lowers the probability of re-employment. Hence, in so far as wage adjustment under imperfect competition turns on changes in the reservation wage, the adjustment must be less than would obtain under competitive arrangements because it will entail a rise in unemployment.)

Furthermore, although these results must be qualified by our questioning of the Nash solution, the questioning has supplied an insight regarding the likely role of conventions in wage determination. This is potentially rather important. It reinforces the conclusions from Chapter 6 and suggests that the actual behaviour of wages and prices is likely to depend on conventions. Thus, in so far as governments are concerned to influence the supply side of the economy, then they will have to venture into what is an unfamiliar policy terrain. The other side of this observation is that it would not be at all surprising to find that the sources of extraneous information differed across countries and so these differences might help explain the different macroeconomic performances of otherwise similar economies.

7.5 Hysteresis and all that

The conclusions of the previous two sections rest in part on the assumption that unions are willing to trade employment for wages. At first sight this seems a plausible assumption, but from a dynamic perspective it is not so obvious that a union would behave in this manner. In particular, once we allow for the possibility that the probability of re-employment in a future period falls if you are unemployed in the current period, then matters will be rather different. This can be easily appreciated if we suppose that the union wishes to maximize the present discounted value of the representative worker's expected utility over a number of periods, as in

$$\Sigma \theta^i E(U_i) = \Sigma \theta^i \{ p_i [U(W/P_i) - D] + (1-p_i)[U(A_i)] \} \quad (7.11)$$

where θ is the discount factor, the one period expected utility is taken from equation 7.1 and p_i is the probability of employment in period i.

The maximization of this more complicated objective function will yield the same behaviour as the one-period maximization problem when the probability of unemployment in one period is independent of the probability of unemployment in a previous period. In these circumstance, this period's choice of wages and unemployment has no effect on future options and so the maximization of 7.11 will be achieved by maximizing each period's expected utility. However, when unemployment in this period affects the likelihood of unemployment in the next period then unemployment in this period will reduce the expected utility of future periods and so the maximization one period expected utility will not be part of the maximization of 7.11. The maximization of 7.11 will take account of how unemployment now undermines expected utilities in the future and so trade less unemployment now for lower wages in the present.

Before I develop the implications of this greater reluctance to accept unemployment, it is probably sensible to say something about why the probability of future employment might depend negatively on previous unemployment.

A variety of mechanisms have been suggested in the literature. To mention two that spring to mind. There is one which fits the union context well that has become known as the insider-outsider model. It suggests that effective membership of a union depends on employment, otherwise subscriptions lapse, attendance at meetings falls away, etc. Consequently, since the union only attends to the interests of its membership, individuals will not want to become unemployed because this will mean that the union ceases to take account of their interests in wage negotiations. Another draws attention to the need for employment experience to keep human capital skills up to snuff. Under this version, a period of unemployment leads to the atrophy of human capital and makes the person increasingly unemployable in the future.

Let us work for illustrative purposes with the insider-outsider version. The maximization of 7.11 is actually quite complicated. But, it is natural to suppose that the greater reluctance to accept unemployment leads to greater wage flexibility. In effect, union membership gives individuals access to some rents which come from bargaining with the employer, and so workers prefer not to share these with others during a boom by allowing employment to increase and likewise wish to avoid losing employment during a downturn because this will undermine their ability to enjoy a share of these rents in the future. Hence, the dynamic perspective qualifies our earlier results with respect to wage stickiness.

However, the picture is rather more complicated than this. The mechanisms which help to create this wage sensitivity also have the paradoxical effect of introducing a rather different sort of problem for employment in the economy. Any errors which lead to employment deviations will tend to have a persistent effect – the phenomena of hysteresis. To see the complete picture here, consider Figure 7.8.

I shall assume that the union objective in this dynamic context becomes the equivalent of preserving current employment, provided the wage does not fall below the reservation value. Thus, when the demand for labour varies between L_0 and L_1 and the current membership is N_0, the wage set by the union fluctuates between $(W/P)_0$ and $(W/P)_1$. To contrast with the analysis of section 7.3, the shift in demand to L_0 is not met with an unchanged wage because the union members realize that the fall in employment to N_1 will undermine some of their capacities to gain employment in the future. The membership would become N_1 and when the labour demand shifts out again the employment level of N_0 would not be regained, and instead the wage rate

Figure 7.8 Hysteresis in an insider/outsider model

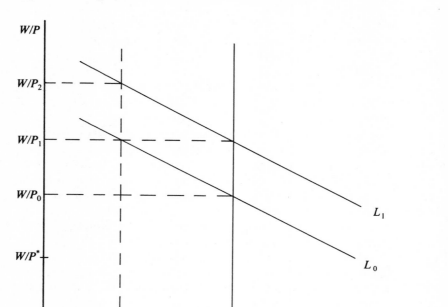

would rise to $(W/P)_2$. However, consider what happens when the union makes a mistake with respect to the cyclical conjuncture. It believes labour demand is at L_1 when in fact it is at L_0. The union sets the wage at $(W/P)_1$ but this means that the firm sets employment at N_1. Union membership contracts to N_1 and thereafter variations in labour demand produce, in the absence of any further errors, employment at N_1.

The possibility of hysteresis provides a timely reminder that even when wages are cyclically responsive in models of imperfect competition, there may remain a role for supply side policies because mistakes may occur and they are not necessarily easily reversed.

7.6 Efficiency Wages

The efficiency wage hypothesis turns on the idea that the effort expended by a worker depends positively on the wage that he or she receives. Thus, we can write that effective labour input E equals $E(W/P)L$, where E gives the relation between effort and wage per worker with $E' > 0$. Modifying the real revenue function to take account of the fact that output now depends on effective labour input, profit maximization entails

$$\max R(E,B) - (W/P)L \qquad (7.12)$$

Assume that the firm sets both the wage and the level of employment. So, partially differentiating this respect to L and W/P and setting both equal to 0 entails

$$E(W/P)R_E - W/P = 0$$

and

$$E'R_E - L = 0$$

Solving these two first order conditions yields a choice of wage given by

$$(W/P)E'(W/P)/E(W/P) = 1 \qquad (7.13)$$

That is, the profit maximizing wage is the one that makes the elasticity of effort with respect to the wage equal to 1. In other words, the wage is chosen to minimize the wage costs per unit of effective labour and then labour is employed up to the point where this wage is equal to the real marginal revenue product of labour. Changes in B will not affect the choice of wage to minimize wage costs in 7.13 because this depends only on the E function. Thus cyclical changes in the real revenue function produce no change in the wage and only changes in the level of employment.

This is an arresting result, and so it is worth exploring the source of the relation between effort and the wage which is responsible for this result. Originally, the hypothesis was advanced in connection with effort in poor countries where effort was likely to depend on nutrition and nutrition in turn plausibly depends on the real wage. In the context of richer countries, this would be a difficult argument to sustain, but there are a number of alternative explanations of why a similar relation might exist in these countries. I will mention three of them.

With all three explanations, it is helpful to return to some of the issues discussed in section 7.2. First, consider the prisoner's dilemma which arises over workers expending high effort when they are paid a high wage. There we had a discrete choice of either making the effort or not, rather than a continuous range of efforts which is implied by the effort function E. Nevertheless, the similarity is enough to see the general point that the employer can induce workers to expend high effort by offering them a suitably high wage when the game is repeated. The firm can threaten any worker who is caught not expending a high effort with being fired; and the worker will expend the higher effort provided the high wage represents a sufficient premium, given the probability of being caught shirking, over the next best alternative which is available to a worker once fired.

With this line of argument, it should be noted that we expect some response of real wages to changes in demand for labour. For instance, suppose demand falls and unemployment rises because there is no immediate adjustment of the real wage. We should nevertheless expect the real wage to fall eventually because the rise in unemployment reduces the expected value of the workers' next best options once they have been fired and so the wage does not have to be as high to yield the necessary premium to motivate workers to expend a high effort. However, this noted, it is also plain that this real wage response can never be such that unemployment returns to its original level, as one would expect under competitive arrangements. This can be appreciated by reflecting on the fact that unemployment has to rise in some degree to generate a fall in the expected value of the next best alternative to current employment, and without this fall there is no reason for wage offers to fall.

Another explanation of the relation comes from the managerial literature which finds that worker morale both influences productivity and is itself affected by wage rates. To put it plainly, when workers are paid a high wage, they feel good about themselves and this makes them more alert and more creative in ways that raise productivity. In contrast, low wages breed low self-esteem and a lack of creativity. This general line of argument begs a question about what determines the level of wages at which workers switch from low to high morale and it is tempting to make two observations on this. First, that past wage rates (or past rates of change if they have been changing) may provide the best guide to workers to what they expect, so that when these expectations are not met, morale drops. This anchoring of morale in history will for obvious reasons impart inertia to wage movements. Second, workers may seek out comparisons with others and it is when relative wages fall that morale drops. This being the case, we have an interesting coordination problem with two possible equilibria where firms avoid falls in morale. Either all firms lower wages in response to a decline in demand, in which case there is no decline in morale because relative wages have not changed. Or no firm lowers wages and again there is no change and relative wages and morale remain unchanged. One might reasonably surmise that under a decentralized and staggered wage-setting system, the latter is more likely than the former; and in this form it gives a managerial gloss to Keynes's original argument that a concern for relative wages imparts inertia to the level of wages.

One final way of running the argument is to build on the insight that there are elements of bargaining at stake in the wage rate and so wage rates are likely to have normative attributes of 'fairness' and 'unfairness' attached to them. Under this version, effort depends on the perception of 'fairness' or 'unfairness'. As before this begs a question of what wage rate provides the benchmark for judging whether the current one is 'fair' or 'unfair'. And again, the two candidates of historical and relative comparisons suggest themselves with the same implication as before.

In summary, the efficiency wage hypothesis may be appropriate to labour markets where there is no formal bargaining but which nevertheless have features (like those discussed in section 7.2) which undermine the competitive model. Like the earlier bargaining models they provide reasons for expecting that wages may be stickier than what we find in the competitive model.

7.7 Summary

This chapter has presented a variety of imperfectly competitive models of wage determination. They yield a qualified conclusion that real wages will be stickier than we might expect under competitive market clearing conditions. The conclusion is qualified, however, because the determination of wages is likely to depend on the use of conventions and we have only considered the operation of a restricted set of conventions. Those studied in section 7.4 supported this conclusion, but in the case of efficiency wages where considerations of 'fairness' or 'morale' explain the relationship between effort and wage, we saw that it was possible for some conventions to deliver significant wage sensitivity. Thus while there is some support for wage stickiness, the general message is that an understanding of wage behaviour will depend on the precise conventions which are at play in the labour market.

7.8 A Brief Conclusion

There is always a long and a short story. The short story is this. Demand management begins to make sense once the 'problems' of time and social interdependence are admitted – that is, once we do not simplify the future and social interdependence by appealing to jejune versions of rational expectations and models of perfect competition. Furthermore, the 'problems' themselves might also be directly addresed through the development of supply-side policies. Indeed, it is important that we should develop such policies, particularly if we are to cope better with supply shocks. However, we are unlikely to make much progress here until we recognize and understand better the role in economic life played by conventions and the institutions which embody them.

Let me finish by reminding you how I constructed the longer version of this story. First, conventions and rules of thumb are indispensible when forming expectations (see Chapter 5). The rational expectations hypothesis is not enough to determine expectations either when there is learning to be done or when there are multiple rational expectations equilibria. In the case of the former, many learning rules will approximate adaptive expectations; and this expectational scheme empowers demand management over the 'short-run'. In the case of the latter, a convention is a coordinating device which enables equilibrium selection and demand management affects output and employment under some conventions (or other means of selection).

Second, there are two general information difficulties which can contribute to significant nominal wage and price stickiness; and once there is significant nominal stickiness, the argument for demand management is strengthened because nominal shocks produce lasting changes in output and employment (see sections 3.5 and 6.2). One informational problem relates to the difficulty of distinguishing a nominal demand shock from a real one. A system of staggered wage and price setting may emerge as a response to this problem and it will entail a gradual adjustment of nominal wages and prices to nominal shocks (see section 6.5).

The other informational difficulty concerns the behaviour of other agents in the economy. Even when it is known that there has been a nominal demand disturbance (and the first informational problem does not arise), the best response to such a shock will depend on the actions of others. If other agents are not expected to adjust to a nominal shock, then the individual agent will experience the shock as a real one and the degree of nominal price adjustment will then depend on some real price responsiveness. This is where real and nominal price and wage stickiness become connected. Suppose workers and firms realize there has been a nominal shock but do not expect each other to adjust to the shock. Each experiences the shock as a real one. If there is also significant real price stickiness, then neither the firms nor the workers will adjust their prices. Thus we will observe a failure to adjust prices in response to a nominal shock (that is, nominal stickiness) which is rooted in real stickiness and a particular set of (what prove to be rational) expectations. An alternative set of expectations (to wit, the expectation that everyone would adjust) could produce a very different result as this would dramatically increase the incentive for individual firms and workers to adjust their prices and wages (see sections 6.3 and 6.4). This reminds us again of the importance of selection mechanisms when there are many rational expectations equilibria.

How do agents select one rational expectation in such circumstances? Selection involves coordinating your choice with that of other agents and so it will be achieved by the use of shared extraneous information (conventions) and sometimes these conventions get formally embodied in institutions. In particular, one might hypothesize that centralized wage and price-setting institutions are better placed than decentralized ones to select the equilibrium with price adjustment simply because the choice of equilibrium can be explicitly addressed under such an arrangement. Under decentralized arrangements a shared convention for price and wage setting could produce the same result and we can see from the connection noted above between real and nominal stickiness that this is more likely when there is significant real responsiveness because such responsiveness would undermine a convention of non-adjustment.

Thus the spotlight moves on to the sources of real wage and price stickiness. (Such stickiness is important, it should be remembered, not only because it connects in the manner I have just sketched with the issue of nominal stickiness and the potential for demand management but also because it affects the behaviour of the economy in response to supply shocks and the argument for supply-side activism.) So why might there be significant real stickinesses? Small 'menu' costs have featured prominently in the explanations offered here (see sections 6.3, 6.4 and 7.3). And the other element of the explanation comes from a recognition that prices and wages are not just set so as to clear the market, they are also set as a result of a bargain that divides a surplus or a 'rent' which can arise in particular economic relationships formed in labour and product markets (see sections 6.6 and 7.2).

In such conditions of 'bargaining', we do not expect prices and wages to be as responsive to real shocks as they would be in competitive markets. This is a qualified expectation because the determination of the wage or the price in these conditions will depend on the precise convention used to settle the wage/price and some conventions can deliver significant flexibility. Nevertheless, setting the qualification on one side for the moment, this insight over bargaining together with the earlier one on centralization suggest that we might expect nominal flexibility either in centralized wage and price systems or in decentralized ones where there are competitive markets because competitive markets increase real flexibilities and, as we have seen, this bolsters nominal responsiveness in the absence of a centralized system. In comparison, wage and price-setting institutions which are decentralized and which are also imperfectly competitive (and are characterized by explicit or implicit bargaining) are the least likely to exhibit nominal flexibility. (Hargreaves Heap, 1991, can be consulted for further arguments in support of this conclusion because the degree of real wage flexibility, under imperfect competition, can itself be positively linked to the existence of centralized/corporatist arrangements.)

This is only a tentative conclusion because we do not understand well the operation of conventions and institutions in labour and product markets. Nevertheless, the prominence given to conventions and institutions in this conclusion is absolutely right because this is the underlaying message that we get from the models of Chapters 5, 6 and 7. The macrobehaviour of the economy depends on its microfoundations and any realistic microfoundations must have a vein of the conventional and institutional running through them.

Some conventions and institutions will yield a supply side of the economy where demand management can be usefully employed. This is an important result, but we should not forget that the invitation to demand management in these circumstances is really only a part of a more general invitation to develop supply-side policies.

7.9 A Brief Guide to the Literature

Solow (1980) provides a very useful survey of the whole area of wage setting. Okun (1975, 1981) is good on the peculiarities of labour markets while McDonald and Solow (1981) are the source for the discussion of the monopoly and Nash bargaining model. Gill (1984) shows how adjustment costs introduce bargaining into almost every economic relationship and Azariadis and Stiglitz (1983) discuss some of the difficulties with writing contracts and provide references to the large contracts literature. Sugden (1990) and Varoufakis (1991) can be consulted for an extended discussion of what is 'wrong' with the Nash solution. Hargreaves Heap (1980) provides an early discussion of hysteresis, and Lindbeck and Snower (1989) are the authorities on insider-outsider models. Leibenstein (1957) provides one of the early efficiency wage models and Yellen (1984) and Katz (1987) contain useful surveys. Finally, Calmfors and Driffill (1988) offer a different argument with respect to and survey of the growing literature which connects macroperformance to institutional arrangements. This literature has grown significantly since I completed this book. Hargreaves Heap (1991) provides an extended discussion of how centralized and corporatist wage setting arrangements affect nominal and real wage rigidity, and thus it constitutes a natural postscript extension to this chapter.

References

Akerlof, George and Yellen, Janet (1985), 'A Near-Rational Model of the Business Cycle with Wage and Price Inertia', *Quarterly Journal of Economics*, **100**, 823–38.

Alchian, Armen (1970), 'Information Costs, Pricing and Resource Unemployment' in E. Phelps (ed.), *Microeconomic Foundations of Employment and Inflation Theory*, London: Macmillan.

Arrow, Kenneth (1959), 'Towards a Theory of Price Adjustment' in M. Abromovitz *et al.* (eds), *The Allocation of Resources: Essays in Honour of Bernard Frances Haley*, Stanford: Stanford University Press.

Azariadis, Costas (1981), 'Self-Fulfilling Prophecies', *Journal of Economic Theory*, **25**, 380–96.

Azariadis, Costas and Stiglitz, Joseph (1983), 'Implicit Contracts and Fixed Price Equilibria', *Quarterly Journal of Economics*, **98**, 1–23.

Bacharach, M. (1976), *Economics and the Theory of Games*, London: Macmillan.

Backus, David and Driffill, John (1985), 'Inflation and Reputation', *American Economic Review*, **75**, 530–8.

Ball, Laurence and Cecchetti, Stephen (1988), 'Imperfect Information and Price Staggering', *American Economic Review*, **78**, 999–1018.

Ball, Laurence, Mankiw, Gregory and Romer, David (1988), 'The New Keynesian Economics and the Output-Inflation Trade-off', *Brookings Papers on Economic Activity*, **I**, 1–79.

Barro, Robert (1974), 'Are Government Bonds Net Wealth?', *Journal of Political Economy*, **82**, 1095–118.

Barro, Robert and Gordon, David (1983), 'Rules, Discretion and Reputation in a Model of Monetary Policy', *Journal of Monetary Economics*, **12**, 101–21.

Barro, Robert and Grossman, Herschel (1971), 'A General Disequilibrium Model of Income and Employment', *American Economic Review*, **61**, 82–93.

Binmore, K. and Dasgupta, P. (1986), *Economic Organisations as Games*, Oxford: Basil Blackwell.

Blanchard, Olivier (1983), 'Price Asynchronization and Price Level Inertia' in R. Dornbusch and M. Simonsen (eds), *Inflation, Debt and Indexation*, Cambridge, Mass: MIT Press.

Blanchard, Olivier and Watson, Michael (1982), 'Bubbles, Rational Expectations, and Financial Markets', in P. Wachtel (ed.), *Crises in the Economic and Financial Structure*, Lexington, Mass: Lexington Books.

Blanchard, Olivier and Kiyotaki, Nobuhiro (1987), 'Monopolistic Competition and the Effects of Aggregate Demand', *American Economic Review*, **77**, 647–66.

Blanchard, O. and Fischer, S. (1989), *Lectures on Macroeconomics*, Cambridge, Mass: MIT Press.

Bray, Margaret (1985), 'Rational Expectations, Information and Asset Markets: An Introduction', *Oxford Economic Papers*, **37**, 161–95.

Buiter, Willem (1980), 'The Macroeconomics of Dr Pangloss: A Critical survey of the New Classical Macroeconomics', *Economic Journal*, **90**, 34–50.

Calmfors, Lars and Driffill, John (1988), 'Bargaining Structure and Macroeconomic Performance; *Economic Policy*, **6**, 14–61.

Carabelli, A. (1988), *On Keynes's Method*, London: Macmillan.

Clower, Robert (1965), 'The Keynesian Counter-Revolution: A Theoretical Approach' in F. Hahn and F. Brechling (eds), *The Theory of Interest Rates*, London: Macmillan.

Cooper, Russell and John, Andrew (1988), 'Coordinating Coordination Failures in Keynesian Models', *Quarterly Journal of Economics*, **53**, 441–63.

Coutts, K., Godley, W. and Nordhaus, W. (1978), *Industrial Pricing in the UK*, Cambridge: Cambridge University Press.

Dornbusch, Rudiger (1976), 'Expectations and Exchange Rate Dynamics', *Journal of Political Economy*, **84**, 1161–76.

Douglas, M. (1982), *In the Active Voice*, London: Routledge & Kegan Paul.

Fitzgibbons, A. (1988), *Keynes's Vision: A New Political Economy*, Oxford: Clarendon Press.

Foster, J. (1987), *Evolutionary Macroeconomics*, London: Allen and Unwin.

Frank, J. (1986), *New Keynesian Economics: Unemployment Search and Contracting*, Brighton: Wheatsheaf.

Friedman, Benjamin (1979), 'Optimal Expectations and the Extreme Information Assumptions of "Rational Expectations" Macromodels', *Journal of Monetary Economics*, **5**, 23–41.

Friedman, M. (1957), *A Theory of the Consumption Function*, New Jersey: Princeton University Press.

Friedman, Milton (1968), 'The Role of Monetary Policy', *American Economic Review*, **58**, 1–17.

Frisch, R. (1933), 'Propagation Problems and Impulse Problems in Dynamic Economics' in *Economic Essays in Honour of Gustav Cassel*, London.

Frydman, R. and Phelps, E. (1983), *Individual Forecasting and Aggregate Outcomes*, Cambridge: Cambridge University Press.

Geanakoplos, J. (1987), 'Overlapping Generations Model of General

Equilibrium', in J. Eatwell, M. Milgate and P. Newman (eds), *The New Palgrave: A Dictionary of Economics*, volume 3, London: Macmillan.

Geanakoplos, J. and Polemarchakis, H. (1986), 'Walrasian Indeterminacy and Keynesian Macroeconomics', *Review of Economic Studies*, **53**, 755–79.

Giddens, A. (1979), *Central Problems in Social Theory*, London: Macmillan.

Gill, Flora (1984), 'The Costs of Adjustment and the Invisible Hand; with Special Reference to the Labour Market', *Economie Appliquee*, **37**, 523–41.

Gordon, Robert (1990), 'What is the New-Keynesian Economics?', *Journal of Economic Literature*, September, 1115–71.

Grandmont, Jean-Michel (1985), 'On Endogenous Competitive Business Cycles', *Econometrica*, **53**, 995–1045.

Grossman, Sanford and Stiglitz, Joseph (1980), 'On the Impossibility of Informationally Efficient Markets', *American Economic Review*, **70**, 393–408.

Hahn, F. (1980), *Money and Inflation*, Oxford: Basil Blackwell.

Hahn, Frank and Solow, Robert (1989), 'Is Wage Flexibility a Good Thing?' in W. Beckerman (ed.), *Wage Rigidity and Unemployment*, London: Duckworth.

Hargreaves Heap, Shaun (1980), 'Choosing the Wrong "Natural" Rate: Accelerating Inflation or Decelerating Employment and Growth', *Economic Journal*, **90**, 611–20.

Hargreaves Heap, S. (1989), *Rationality in Economics*, Oxford: Basil Blackwell.

Hargreaves Heap, Shaun (1991), 'Institutions and macroeconomic performance', *UEA Economics Research Centre Discussion Paper*.

Hicks, J. (1937), 'Mr Keynes and the "Classics": A Suggested Interpretation', *Econometrica*, **5**, 147–59.

Johnson, Harry (1976), 'The Monetary Approach to the Balance of Payments', in J. Frenkel and H. Johnson (eds), *The Monetary Approach to the Balance of Payments*, London: Allen and Unwin.

Katz, Lawrence (1987), 'Efficiency Wage Theories: A Partial Evaluation', *NBER Macroeconomics Annual*, 1987, 235–76.

Keynes, J. (1936), *The General Theory of Employment, Interest and Money*, London: Macmillan.

Kreps, David and Wilson, Robert (1982a), 'Sequential Equilibria', *Econometrica*, **50**, 863–94.

Kreps, David and Wilson, Robert (1982b), 'Reputation and Imperfect Information', *Journal of Economic Theory*, **27**, 253–79.

Kydland, Finn and Prescott, Edward (1977), 'Rules Rather than Discretion: the Inconsistency of Optimal Plans', *Journal of Political Economy*, **85**, 473–91.

Kydland, Finn and Prescott, Edward (1982), 'Time to Build and Aggregate Fluctuations', *Econometrica*, **50**, 1345–70.

Laidler, David (1984), 'The "Buffer Stock" Notion in Monetary Economics', *Economic Journal Conference Papers*, **94**, 17–34.

Layard, Richard and Nickell, Steven (1986), 'Unemployment in Britain', *Economica*, **53**, S121–70.

Leibenstein, H. (1957), 'The Theory of Underdevelopment in Densely Populated Backward Areas' in H. Leibenstein (ed.), *Economic Backwardness and Growth*, New York: Wiley.

Leijonhufvud, A. (1968), *On Keynesian Economics and the Economics of Keynes*, London: Oxford University Press.

Lindbeck, A. and Snower, D. (1989), *The Insider-Outsider Theory of Employment and Unemployment*, Cambridge, Mass: MIT Press.

Lucas, Robert (1973), 'Some International Evidence on Output-Inflation Trade-offs', *American Economic Review*, **63**, 326–34.

Lucas, R. (1981), *Studies in Business Cycle Theory*, Cambridge, Mass: MIT Press.

Lucas, Robert and Rapping, Leonard (1969), 'Real Wages, Employment and Inflation', *Journal of Political Economy*, **77**, 721–54.

McCallum, Bennett (1989), 'Real Business Cycle Models' in R. Barro (ed.), *Modern Business Cycle Theory*, Oxford: Basil Blackwell.

McDonald, Ian and Solow, Robert (1981), 'Wage Bargaining and Employment', *American Economic Review*, **71**, 896–908.

Mankiw, Gregory (1985), 'Small Menu Costs and Large Business Cycles: A Macroeconomic Model of Monopoly', *Quarterly Journal of Economics*, **100**, 529–37.

Malinvaud, E. (1977), *The Theory of Unemployment Reconsidered*, Oxford: Basil Blackwell.

Meade, J. (1951), *The Balance of Payments*, London: Oxford University Press.

Mundell, Robert (1963), 'Capital Mobility and Stabilization Policy under Fixed and Floating Exchange Rates', *Canadian Journal of Economics and Political Science*, **29**, 4, 475–85.

Muth, John (1961), 'Rational Expectations and the Theory of Price Movements', *Econometrica*, **29**, 315–35.

O'Donnell, R. (1989), *Keynes: Philosophy, Politics and Economics*, London: Macmillan.

Okun, Arthur (1975), 'Inflation: its Mechanics and Welfare Costs', *Brookings Papers on Economic Activity*, **2**, 352–90.

Okun, A. (1981), *Prices and Quantities: A Macroeconomic Analysis*, Washington: Brookings Institution.

Oswald, Andrew (1985), 'The Economic Theory of Trade Unions: An Introductory Survey', *Scandinavian Journal of Economics*, **87**, 160–93.

Patinkin, D. (1965), *Money, Interest and Prices*, 2nd ed., New York: Harper and Row.

Phelps, E. (ed.) (1970), *The Microeconomic Foundations of Employment and Inflation Theory*, New York: Norton.

Rasmusen, E. (1989), *Games and Information*, Oxford: Basil Blackwell.

Rotemberg, Julio (1982), 'Monopolistic Price Adjustment and Aggregate Output', *Review of Economic Studies*, **49**, 517–31.

Rotemberg, Julio (1987), 'The New Keynesian Microfoundations', *NBER Macroeconomics Annual*, **2**, 69–104.

Rotemberg, Julio and Saloner, Garth (1986), 'A Supergame-Theoretic Model of Price Wars during Booms', *American Economic Review*, **76**, 390–407.

Rubinstein, A. (1982), 'Perfect Equilibrium in a Bargaining Model', *Econometrica*, **53**, 1151–72.

Samuelson, Paul (1958), 'An Exact Consumption Loan Model of Interest, With or Without the Social Contrivance of Money', *Journal of Political Economy*, **66**, 467–82.

Sargent, Thomas and Wallace, Neil (1975), '"Rational" Expectations, the Optimal Monetary Instrument, and the Optimal Money Supply Rule', *Journal of Political Economy*, **83**, 241–54.

Selten, R. (1975), 'Re-examination of the Perfectness Concept for Equilibrium in Extensive Games', *International Journal of Game Theory*, **4**, 22–5.

Solow, Robert (1980), 'On Theories of Unemployment', *American Economic Review*, **70**, 1–11.

Sugden, R. (1986), *The Economics of Rights, Cooperation and Welfare*, Oxford: Basil Blackwell.

Sugden, Robert (1990), 'Convention, Creativity and Conflict' in Y. Varoufakis and D. Young (eds), *Conflict in Economics*, Hemel Hempstead: Harvester Wheatsheaf.

Taylor, John (1979), 'Staggered Wage Setting in a Macro Model', *American Economic Review*, **69**, 108–13.

Taylor, John (1980), 'Aggregate Dynamics and Staggered Contracts', *Journal of Political Economy*, **88**, 1–23.

Tirole, J. (1989), *The Theory of Industrial Organisation*, Cambridge, Mass: MIT Press.

Tobin, James (1975), 'Keynesian Models of Recession and Depression', *American Economic Review*, **65**, 195–202.

Varoufakis, Y. (1991), *Rational Conflict*, Oxford: Basil Blackwell.

Yellen, Janet (1984), 'Efficiency Wage Models of Unemployment', *American Economic Review*, **74**, 200–5.

Index